Move over Dr. Spock. Here is a practical guide that will make a difference in my own parenting.

Becoming the
PARENT
God Wants You to Be

Becoming the
PARENT
God Wants You to Be

DR. KEVIN LEMAN
WITH DAVE & NETA JACKSON

NAVPRESS
BRINGING TRUTH TO LIFE
NavPress Publishing Group
P.O. Box 35001, Colorado Springs, Colorado 80935

OUR GUARANTEE TO YOU

We believe so strongly in the message of our books that we are making this quality guarantee to you. If for any reason you are disappointed with the content of this book, return the title page to us with your name and address and we will refund to you the list price of the book. To help us serve you better, please briefly describe why you were disappointed. Mail your refund request to: NavPress, P.O. Box 35002, Colorado Springs, CO 80935.

The Navigators is an international Christian organization. Our mission is to reach, disciple, and equip people to know Christ and to make Him known through successive generations. We envision multitudes of diverse people in the United States and every other nation who have a passionate love for Christ, live a lifestyle of sharing Christ's love, and multiply spiritual laborers among those without Christ.

NavPress is the publishing ministry of The Navigators. NavPress publications help believers learn biblical truth and apply what they learn to their lives and ministries. Our mission is to stimulate spiritual formation among our readers.

FOR A FREE CATALOG OF
NAVPRESS BOOKS & BIBLE STUDIES,
CALL 1-800-366-7788 (USA)
OR 1-416-499-4615 (CANADA)

This book is affectionately dedicated to the six loves of my life—
my wife, Sande, and our five children, Holly, Kris, Kevin II, Hannah,
and Lauren. It is a privilege to be your husband and father.
I love you all more than words can express.
Thanks for all you've given me.

Contents

Preface

I come to you as a psychologist who has written eighteen books and been on TV talk shows all across the country—but mostly I come to you as a daddy. A daddy who has helped raise five children, and, I don't mind telling you, five pretty good ones!

There's a lot of confusing information out there these days. Walk into any bookstore, secular or sanctified, and you can stagger out with a dozen conflicting books on parenting. I'm concerned by the popular wisdom that says parents shouldn't stifle little Percival's right to choose how he's brought up (read: the child is in control). And I'm equally concerned by a popular movement among well-meaning Christians that says parents should decide when baby Percival should be hungry, sleepy, or quiet, and that makes every parenting issue one of rebellion versus instant obedience (read: the parent is in total control).

Both extremes miss the point. The issue is not who's going to win the power struggle (though it might feel like that at times). The real issue is how we parents can use our God-given authority in a way that assures our children that they are loved and at the same time helps them be accountable for their own choices and actions. How can we create a sense of belonging by teaching our children to give back to the family—as they used to do when they were an essential part of the agrarian society—in contrast to encouraging the gimme, gimme, gimme attitude so prevalent in North American society? How can we instill in them a sense of their own worth—and the worth of others in God's sight—and give them hope that they can "make it" even when they make mistakes?

Big questions, yes—but I'm convinced this is not rocket science. That's why I felt compelled to create a curriculum that would give you, as parents, specific ways to use your authority in a healing manner, with loving discipline, as you bring up obedient, confident, responsible children. A parenting curriculum that makes sense! As you work through this study with other parents, I hope you all will discover that what your child needs is not a perfect parent, but a *good* parent. A parent like you, who is *Becoming the Parent God Wants You to Be*.

Resources

The topics we'll tackle in this study guide are developed more fully in several of my previous books. It would be great to have copies of these available for those who want to explore a topic in greater detail.

Bringing Up Kids Without Tearing Them Down
Nashville, Tenn.: Thomas Nelson Publishers, Inc., 1995.

Keeping Your Family Together When the World Is Falling Apart
Colorado Springs, Colo.: Focus on the Family, 1993.

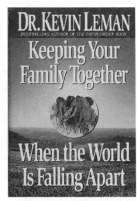

Living in a Stepfamily Without Getting Stepped On
Nashville, Tenn.: Thomas Nelson Publishers, Inc., 1994.

The New Birth Order Book
Grand Rapids, Mich.: Fleming H. Revell, 1998.

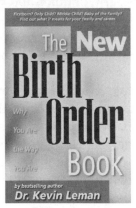

Making Children Mind Without Losing Yours
Grand Rapids, Mich.: Fleming H. Revell, 1984.

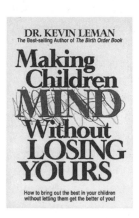

Winning the Rat Race
Nashville, Tenn.: Fleming Thomas Nelson Publishers, 1996.

Introduction

One thing I'll say for my parents, John and May Leman: There was never a day in my life that I didn't feel loved. My dad, a dry cleaner, had an eighth-grade education; he didn't know a thing about parenting, but he knew an awful lot about being a dad. My mom was a registered nurse. She knew a lot about giving.

And both of them knew that real love requires discipline.

Too many parents live in constant fear that they're going to do something to mess up their children. One mistake and, bam! their child will join the skinheads or the punkers. But that's not the way it works. God isn't expecting perfection from us. That's why His best gifts involve grace, mercy, and forgiveness. Perfection is overrated, anyway. It makes other people shy away from you (perfectionists are hard to be around), and our children aren't fooled, anyway: they *know* we're not perfect and lose respect for us if we think we're right all the time.

Becoming the Parent God Wants You to Be is designed to help you as parents create in your children a self-image that's healthy and rooted in Christ, to strengthen that character, and finally to road-test it. And that's the tough part for us as parents. Along the way I'll talk about the seeds of self-esteem, the ABCs: Acceptance. Belonging. Competence. Those are the things that you need to worry about as a parent. Are you accepting the differences in your children? Do you treat them differently? Do your children feel like they belong? And by the time your children join the hormone group—ages twelve, thirteen, and fourteen—will they see themselves as capable of doing something? Will they see themselves as valued people, as contributors to their family?

Want to try an experiment? Do you have access to a two-year-old child? Extend your arms toward the toddler and simply say, "Come here." What happens? The child heads north when you expected a more southerly route! But if you'll do the same thing and walk backwards, you will see the child approach you. Psychologically, that's the environment you want to create—one that's inviting, isn't threatening, and says you're approachable.

Remember when we were kids and used to play ball in the vacant lot? Did you have a Harold? He would show up in his brown oxfords with his pants pulled up to his armpits, and couldn't catch a ball if he had to. We used to choose up teams, and it would go something like this:

"I'll take Jamie."

"And I'll take Moonhead."

"I'll take Cub."

"Okay, I'll take him, and you take Harold."

"Oh no, you take Harold. We had him yesterday. You get Harold today."

Nevertheless, Harold came around, day after day after day. He wanted to belong. You know, we were mean to that little kid, and I really do feel badly. But there's a lesson in his story for all of us. He demonstrates how much any child wants to belong.

Here's what I want to communicate to you parents. If you have a loving Christian home, if your children feel prized and special, and if you hold them accountable for what they do in life, they will have very little motivation to go out and attach themselves to a gang or some other destructive group that's going to tear their lives apart. So I want to encourage you: You can be a good parent, in healthy authority over your children, loving them and letting them know they are special. The good news for us parents is that God didn't put us on this earth for our children to walk over us. We need to function as parents so kids learn that life doesn't revolve around them.

What children need today are not perfect parents, but good parents. A *good* parent is, among other things, one who allows himself or herself a margin of error. Dad realizes there is forgiveness and redemption, even if he occasionally blows it big-time. When Mom loses it, she knows there are some basic principles to return to. At the heart of this "real-life parenting" is Reality Discipline: a consistent, decisive, and respectful way for parents to love and discipline their children. Notice that I said "discipline" and not "punishment." And notice that I also said "love" and not "smother with love."

These principles, I believe, can be summed up in the following words from the apostle Paul in Ephesians 6:1-4 (TLB):

> Children, obey your parents; this is the right thing to do because God has placed them in authority over you. Honor your father and mother. This is the first of God's Ten Commandments that ends with a promise. And this is the promise: that if you honor your father and mother, yours will be a long life, full of blessing. And now a word to you parents. Don't keep on scolding and nagging your children, making them angry and resentful. Rather, bring them up with the loving discipline the Lord himself approves, with suggestions and godly advice.

What does it take to turn out a great child? Not a perfect parent, but a *good* parent—someone like you.

How to Use This Book

I'd enjoy nothing more than to get together with you in Manhattan or Minot or Memphis or Melbourne and take you personally on this journey to "becoming the parent God wants you to be." But "Reality Discipline" applies to my own life as well, and the reality is I can't be in thirteen places at once. Even if I could, it wouldn't leave me any time to fool around with my gorgeous wife, Sande, or figure out how to keep up with my six-year-old. Like I said, we have five children ages twenty-five, twenty-four, twenty, eleven, and six.

So that brings up the question of how to use this book?

- **With a group,** designate a facilitator (better yet, a couple or a threesome who can share preparation and presentation). The facilitator doesn't have to be an "expert." (I'm still learning; why not you?) It's okay to have questions, share your own parenting challenges, and be part of the learning process. After all, that's what the body of Christ is all about: encouraging one another to "grow up in Him."

- **As a couple or couples,** take turns in providing leadership for either alternating sessions or sections within each session. This should not require any advance preparation because the steps are fairly self-explanatory. Proceed at your own pace. However, if there is opportunity, consider joining with another couple to go through the course. You may benefit greatly by sharing your experiences and insights without losing the intimacy of a truly small setting.

- **By yourself,** it is possible to get 88.6 percent (well, more or less) of the value of this course that you would in a small group. However, why not check around for a few other parents who might enjoy studying this with you?

Each session conforms roughly to the following format:

1. I'll introduce a new facet of becoming the parent God wants you to be.

2. We will dig into the Bible to get some solid foundation from God's Word.

3. I'll give you some practical input from the "Dr. Kevin Leman School of Parenting" on the topic.

4. We'll examine how these principles work in typical family situations.

5. You can apply what you've learned to your own parenting needs.

Watch for the following elements within each section that announce various activities.

 Brainstorm ideas that may apply.

 Use a videotape as a supplement to this session.

 Write responses or fill in answers.

 Examine these ideas.

Divide the whole group into smaller groups.

 Continue in small groups for this activity.

 Reconvene the whole group to carry out the next exercise. (This instruction will not be given when it is obvious that the whole group should reconvene to consider further material.)

 Pray with each other about . . .

If you are studying this course as a group, ways to present the "content" sections will be the biggest challenge. Here are a few ideas how this might work. Try to mix and match a few of these suggestions just to keep things interesting.

1. Familiarize yourself with a content section and present it in your own words. Ask the other facilitator(s) to do the same with other sections, taking turns throughout the session. This also could be a mix of presenting some material in your own words and reading the illustrations or stories.

2. Simply read the content sections aloud, pausing along the way for questions or discussion.

3. Ask various participants to read the content section(s) aloud for the rest of the group.

4. Ask participants to read the content parts of the session *ahead of time* in preparation for the next session. During the actual session, ask various participants to "recap" what the content section is about, then move into activities or discussion.

Be sensitive to the fact that there may be one or two parents who feel uncomfortable reading aloud or being called on. That's okay. The idea is to help folks get as comfortable as they can be. If you sense some uneasiness, change your approach or feel free to shuttle people around to different groups. You also might want to partner with one of the people who feels uncomfortable.

Note: What works best for your group will depend on the size of the group (two? four? twelve? twenty-five?) and the style you and your co-facilitators feel most comfortable using.

Resources

Each of you will want to have your own copy of this study guide. Many of the activities (self-tests, choices, journaling, and so on) can be done right in this book.

In many of the sessions, you will note places where segments can be used from my video series, *Bringing Up Kids Without Tearing Them Down*, Published by Dallas Christian Video. These are available from "Couples of Promise," P.O. Box 35370, Tucson, Arizona 85740, or call 1-800-770-3830. The eight-part video series "Bringing Up Kids Without Tearing Them Down" includes the following programs:

1. "The Seeds of Self-Esteem"
2. "The Three Basic Types of Parents"
3. "How to Be in Healthy Authority over Your Child"
4. "Why Kids Misbehave (and what you can do about it)"
5. "How to Make Your Child Feel Special"
6. "The Powerful Secrets of Reality Discipline"
7. "Living in a Stepfamily (without getting stepped on)"
8. "Keeping Your Family Together When the World Is Falling Apart"

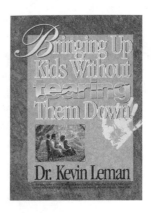

Raising Successful & Confident Kids
Why Kids Misbehave,
Living in a Stepfamily
How to Get Kids to Do What You Want
Them to Do

Keeping the Promise

In addition, my video curriculum for couples, "Keeping the Promise" (Dallas Christian Video), or several individual videos on parenting could be great resources for your study.

And don't forget to look for the suggestions of additional resources at the end of each session.

Well, that's it. Let's get started down the path to *Becoming the Parent God Wants You to Be.*

What Is Godly Parenting?

In *The Birth Order Book*, I reprinted a personal ad I had clipped out of a daily newspaper. It went like this:[1]

> CHRISTIAN, blond, blue eyes, 5'2", 100 lbs., prof., cauc/female, no depend., wishes to meet Protestant Christian, prof. man in 30s with college degree who has compassion for animals and people, loves nature, exercise and phy. fitness (no team sports), music and dance, church and home life. Desire nonsmoker/nondrinker, slender, 5'7"-6', lots of head hair, no chest hair, intelligent, honest and trustworthy, sense of humor, excellent communicator of feelings, very sensitive, gentle, affectionate, androgynous attitude about roles, giving, encouraging and helpful to others, no temper or ego problems, secure within and financially, health conscious, neat and clean, extremely considerate and dependable. I believe in old-fashioned morals and values. If you do too, and are interested in a possible Christian commitment, write P.O. Box 82533. Please include a recent color photo and address.

Let me take a walk on the limb of life and make the guess that this woman will be single a long time.

Unfortunately, babies don't read the want ads before they're born, but many first-time parents carry similarly impossible expectations for their children—and for themselves. We all want to be good parents, and we all want to have delightful children, but being a *godly* parent doesn't mean you need to have perfect children! If it did, how could God be perfect, given all His wayward children? And godly parenting doesn't mean you have to raise your children just like someone else thinks you should—whether that other person is your parent, your neighbor, or some "expert" like me. Sure, weigh the good suggestions and put them into practice. (I'll give you a few myself.) But believe me, when you feel the heat being turned up on you to be a perfect parent, your kids are the ones likely to get scorched.

Godly parenting is not the same as perfectionism, either for you or for your children. Always be aware that there is a vast difference between having standards of excellence and putting too much pressure on your children or yourself to be perfect or to outperform everyone else. (We'll look again at this performance pressure in session 12.)

Let's take a minute to see how much pressure you feel (or put on your kids) to be perfect.

Working by yourself, check off the numbers of the statements below that best describe the way you approach things. Then go over the statements again and mark an **E** beside the statements that you think reflect **Excellence** and a **P** beside those that reflect **Perfectionism**. Check yourself against the answer key on page 34.

EXCELLENCE VERSUS PERFECTIONISM

_____ 1. I encourage my children to do the best they possibly can.

_____ 2. I try to motivate my kids by telling them that "winners never lose, and losers never win."

_____ 3. My self-worth comes primarily from the things I do well.

_____ 4. When my children disappoint me, I get depressed and feel like a failure as a parent.

_____ 5. I've made some mistakes with my children, but I've learned from those mistakes and feel like a better parent.

_____ 6. I encourage my children to try new things, even if they fail at half of them. How else can they discover what they can do?

_____ 7. I expect my children to be the best at whatever they do.

_____ 8. When my children disappoint me, we deal with it and move on.

_____ 9. I encourage my children to stick with the things they know they can do, because I don't want them to suffer the indignity of failure.

_____ 10. My children know that in our competitive society it's the gold medal that counts; silver or bronze is a booby prize.

_____ 11. I tell my children they're really competing against themselves, and they should be satisfied when they know they've done their best.

_____ 12. Sometimes I've blown it with the kids, and I'm afraid they're going to hate me for it.

_____ 13. My self-worth is based on my integrity as a person.

_____ 14. I support my children for playing on the team, whether or not the team wins the game.

 As a supplement to this session, view "The Powerful Secrets of Reality Discipline" on the videotape *Bringing Up Kids Without Tearing Them Down,* © 1994 by Dallas Christian Video.

How God Helps Us Face Life

The bottom line is godly parenting means treating your children the way God treats us, His children. He lovingly helps us make wise decisions about the realities of life.

One of the most moving stories in the Bible is that of the prodigal son. We most often consider it in terms of spiritual conversion. The impulsive, rebellious young man who has ventured far from home and "right living" finally comes to his senses, repents, and returns to seek his father's forgiveness. Throughout the story, it is clear that the father represents God, and we are moved as we identify with the wayward son.

But the story also holds a wealth of information in terms of studying *how* the father parented his son, information we can consider in understanding how God parents us.

 Divide into groups according to the age of your oldest child or the child with whom you feel most challenged as a parent. Read together Luke 15:11-24, then discuss the following questions.

1. What do you think would have happened if the father had gone out immediately after the son left and dragged him home by his left ear?

2. What part did the father play in administering justice or punishment to the son?

3. What measures did the father take to prevent his son from failing? How important do you think it was to the father to prevent his son from failing?

4. How did the son's attitude and actions affect the father's authority in the home?

5. How do you think the father felt as his son chose a dangerous and sinful path? How do you think the father felt when he had been gone for a long time?

6. In what ways did the father allow his feelings to influence his responses toward his son?

7. What differences do you note in the relationships between the prodigal son and his father and between you and your child? In this regard, review each of the previous questions.

 Reconvene in the large group and consider the following thoughts about Reality Discipline.

Reality Discipline

The process of learning how to face life is what I call Reality Discipline, and I believe that it partially describes how our loving, heavenly Father cares for us.

When you use the concepts of Reality Discipline, you know that your child won't make all the right decisions and that you need to give him or her freedom to fail. Nevertheless, you are positive that your child will make more wise decisions than poor ones as he or she learns to be accountable and responsible through self-discipline.

Many psychologists and child-rearing specialists believe in discipline, accountability, responsibility, and helping children make wise decisions. But I am convinced that the distinctives of Reality Discipline can benefit any home where children live. These distinctives include:

Note-it

Commandment I:
My hands are small; please don't expect perfection whenever I make a bed, draw a picture, or throw a ball. My legs are short; please slow down so that I can keep up with you.

1. Parents don't seek to punish. Instead, they try to discipline, train, and teach.

2. If punishment, pain, or some kind of consequence is involved, the parent is not doing it or causing it arbitrarily—reality is. Your child is facing the logical consequences of his or her behavior and learning how the real world works.

Some of the benefits are:

1. Reality Discipline helps prevent inconsistent meandering between authoritarianism and permissiveness. Most parents know instinctively that they should use their authority wisely—being in charge but reasonable and fair. Avoiding the extremes of authoritarianism or permissiveness is best done through Reality Discipline.

2. Reality Discipline teaches accountability and responsibility in ways that will stick. Children learn through making their own decisions and experiencing their own mistakes and failures, as well as successes.

3. Reality Discipline helps prevent the Super Parent Syndrome. If you are using Reality Discipline concepts at all, they will automatically keep you from making the four key mistakes of a Super Parent. The Big Four occur in all kinds of homes, but I have found that Christian families are particularly susceptible. Super Moms and Super Dads often get trapped into the following four kinds of faulty reasoning:[2]

> 1. I own my children.
> 2. I am judge and jury.
> 3. My children can't fail.
> 4. I am the boss—what I say goes.

All four of these erroneous ideas smack of authoritarianism—the style of parenting that is long on control but short on love and support. (We'll look at these parenting styles more closely in session 3.) The authoritarian parent is "in charge" and runs things with an "infallible" and firm hand. It's easy to slip into this kind of thinking when you believe you are doing God's will as you train up your child in the way God wants him to go (as Proverbs 22:6 instructs us). That's why I believe parents should be aware of the four pitfalls of the Super Parent Syndrome. Let's look at these more closely.

Note-it

Commandment II:
My eyes have not seen the world as yours have; please let me explore safely. Don't restrict me unnecessarily.

1. We Don't Own Our Children

We all need to be reminded that our children belong to the Lord Himself. He has given them to us "on loan," with specific guidelines in His Word for the training and enrichment of their lives. Believing this may have been the one thing that gave the father of the prodigal son the strength to let his son go even though he undoubtedly ached as he foresaw the danger and pain ahead. During that time period, if the boy had been a servant rather than a son, he would have been considered property, and the father would have had the "right" to prevent his departure.

When we slip into the Super Parent Syndrome, we can try so hard and get so wrapped up in our children that we act as though we possess them. Reality Discipline, on the other hand, is designed to help you strike a balance that gives your child the security of warmth and love but also gives him or her freedom to make decisions; you can seek to give firm guidance, not to own or control.[3]

Note-it

Commandment III: Housework will always be there. I'm only little for such a short time—please take time to explain things to me about this wonderful world, and do so willingly.

 In the large group, briefly consider the story of the prodigal son in light of this Super Parent pitfall.

■ What might the father have done had he thought he owned his children?

 Working individually, describe the last situation in which you were tempted by this Super Parent trap.

■ How did I act as though I owned my children?

2. We're Not Their Judge and Jury

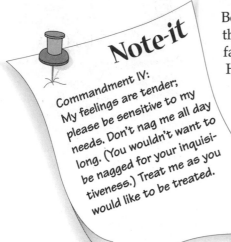

Because we do not own our children, it follows that we are certainly not their judge and jury. In fact, we all know that God is the only judge, and He will judge us *all* someday. Yes, we have authority over our children which we must exercise with love and tenderness. And we must make fair and wise judgments between one thing and another every day. But exercising wisdom is very different from passing down judgments on our children, even though they often try to involve us in doing just that. It is often tempting to step in and solve their problems.

For example, let's look in on Ryan and Michael, ages six and eight. They have been scrapping and fighting after going to bed. Dad has already come in three times and told them to settle down. But Ryan and Michael keep wrestling, arguing, and carrying on. Finally, Ryan (the six-year-old) starts to cry. That does it. Dad's anger button is pushed, and off he goes into their room, determined to settle this—now!

"All right! Who started it?" Dad is now judge and jury, and he's going to find out just where he should dispense proper punishment.

Ryan and Michael simply point at each other. (What a surprise! Can you really imagine one of the little angels admitting to being guilty?) This makes Dad's judge-and-jury role confusing, so he says, "Now listen up! I've had it with you guys. You do nothing but cause trouble around here. If I hear one more peep from this bedroom, you'll both get a spanking. *Do you understand me?*" Without waiting for a reply, Dad leaves in anger, slamming the bedroom door so hard it shakes the whole house.

Uh-oh. Super Dad to the rescue. He has passed judgment ("You do nothing but cause trouble") and threatened punishment ("you'll both get a spanking"). But he hasn't really helped Ryan and Michael solve their problem. Ironically, while acting as judge and jury, Dad really was being manipulated by his own kids to get him involved in their little hassle. His first mistake was correcting them (ineffectively) three times, causing him to commit his second mistake, getting absolutely enraged and resorting to judgments and arbitrary punishments.

What should Dad have done? If he wanted to bring Reality Discipline to bear, he could have worked out a *logical consequence*, telling the boys they would wind up going to bed earlier the next two nights. Or, since the boys were not able to be together quietly, he could have removed one child from the bedroom and made him sleep somewhere else for the night. (We'll talk about Reality Discipline in more detail in sessions 9 through 12.) Whatever a parent does, he or she should avoid playing judge and jury. Parents are not running a court. They are operating a home where encouragement takes the place of bribes and rewards, and discipline always triumphs over punishment. Don't be a Super Parent who tries to solve all problems by passing judgments and dispensing punishments.

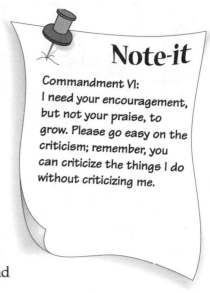

Note-it

Commandment VI:
I need your encouragement, but not your praise, to grow. Please go easy on the criticism; remember, you can criticize the things I do without criticizing me.

To play the Reality Discipline game, however, you need the wisdom to guide your children in making right decisions and letting reality call the shots.[4]

 Consider the story of the prodigal son in light of this Super Parent pitfall.

■ In what ways did the father avoid being judge and jury?

 Describe the last situation in which you were tempted by this Super Parent trap.

■ How did I act as though I was my child's judge and jury?

3. Failure Needn't Be the Worst Fate

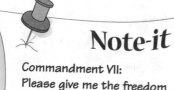

Note-it

Commandment VII:
Please give me the freedom to make decisions concerning myself. Permit me to fail, so that I can learn from my mistakes. Then someday I'll be prepared to make the kinds of decisions life requires of me.

When you slip into Super Parent thinking, failure is not acceptable. Super Parents believe they must not and cannot fail because God is on their side. Naturally enough, they believe their children cannot fail either, and if they do fail, they find this very hard to accept. Children interpret these feelings of disappointment as conditional acceptance, and tension builds.

The truth is that our children *can* fail. In fact, don't tell the Perfection Police, but I believe children *should* fail on occasion because failure can be good for them. Several years ago, Abigail Van Buren picked up "A Child's Ten Commandments to Parents" from my book *Parenthood Without Hassles—Well, Almost* and printed them in her "Dear Abby" column. ("A Child's Ten Commandments to Parents" is reproduced in this session in the Note-its.[5]) Though she was inundated with requests for reprints from her fifty-five million readers, she received more than seven hundred letters from people who didn't like Commandment VII: "Please give me the freedom to make decisions concerning myself. *Permit me to fail,* so that I can learn from my mistakes. Then someday I'll be prepared to make the kinds of decisions life requires of me." Abby commented, "Parents are afraid to let their kids fail."

I'm not saying that children should be failures by habit or that they should learn to be losers in life. I am saying that we can learn through failure. We learn through making our own decisions, and some of those decisions turn out to be mistakes that lead to failure. Failure can be dealt with matter-of-factly and cushioned with love and encouragement from parents.

Note-it

Commandment VIII:
Please don't do things over for me. Somehow that makes me feel that my efforts didn't quite measure up to your expectations. I know it's hard, but please don't try to compare me with my brother or my sister.

I think of Harlan's father, who had been a super athlete in high school and college. Little Harlan tried out for a major division of Little League and didn't make it. He was assigned to a minor league team instead. Without Harlan's permission, his dad went to the coach and tried to talk about it. In the process, his dad lost his temper and there was a shouting match. Some of the parents and most of the team members, all schoolmates of Harlan, heard the entire thing. Harlan was there, too, and was so embarrassed he didn't want to show his face around school for months. He wound up quitting his minor league team and had nothing to do with baseball after that.

Failure is difficult for parents to deal with. Of course, we want our children to succeed in life and be happy, but we need to ask ourselves some questions: When and how did *we* succeed? Didn't we often succeed out of failure? Didn't we go from failure to victory in many phases of our lives?

In fact, when we approach the saving grace of Christ, we do not come out of victory but out of admitting defeat. We are sinners, and we need a savior. As we admit our mistakes and our need for Christ, it is then that we have victory. [6]

 Consider the story of the prodigal son in light of this Super Parent pitfall.

- If the prodigal's father thought failure needed to be avoided at all costs, what might he have tried? What would have been the likely outcome?

 Describe the last situation in which you were tempted by this Super Parent trap.

- How was I afraid of my child's failure? Of my own failure?

4. I Don't Need to Be the Big Boss

The parent who uses Reality Discipline is *in* authority but is never "the boss." With Reality Discipline, you seek to help your child become responsible and accountable for his or her choices, but you do not make his or her decisions. When you slip into Super Parent thinking, you start making decisions for your children because "you know best."

True, every parent knows more than his or her children—most of the time!

There are many situations in which a parent has a good idea what a child should do because the parent has been down that road before.

But Reality Discipline helps you guide the child, not dominate and make all the decisions for the child. Admittedly, it is more trouble to guide a child, but it is infinitely more worthwhile. If a parent makes all of a child's decisions, what happens when that child reaches junior high, high school, college, and adulthood? When I'm counseling young people in difficult situations, I often discover at the root of the problem a parent who still is trying to make decisions for the grown, or practically grown, child.

I often see parents trying to decide for their child what college he or she will attend. Then they decide what job or profession the child should have. Many parents even are involved in deciding whom the child should marry. I'm not saying that parents shouldn't have input about schooling, professions, and marriage partners, but those opinions are far different from control and pressure, which parents too often apply.

Then there is that greatest decision of all. Can any parent make his or her child decide to accept Christ? Not even a Super Parent can pull off that one![7]

 Consider the story of the prodigal son in light of this Super Parent pitfall.

■ What happened to the father's authority when he allowed his son to do something foolish?

Describe the last situation in which you were tempted by this Super Parent trap.

■ What did I do or say that communicated, "I am the boss—what I say goes"?

 Divide again into the small groups created earlier. As a group, come up with a version of the prodigal son story relevant to that age. Incorporate as many of the father's attitudes and approaches as possible with age-appropriate variations. Prepare to tell or act out this new story.

 Reconvene the whole group and share the variations on the prodigal son story the various groups created. Discuss how they express the concept of Reality Discipline.

The Ultimate Goal of Reality Discipline

The most important questions parents ask me are "How do I help my child develop spiritually?" and "How do I enhance my child's relationship with God?"

Be Authentic

The key to answering these questions centers around the Reality Discipline concept of *action, not words.* Children hear many words about God in their home, Sunday school, and church. But too often they don't see much action that seems connected to what they hear. As they grow older, they often have difficulties with the weakness and hypocrisy of the adults around them.

Now there is nothing wrong with being human, but there is a great deal wrong with being hypocritical. I believe that when I freely admit my humanness to my children, I am taking advantage of an ideal opportunity to teach them dependence on the grace of God. As I admit to my children that I don't always have the answers and as I pray with them and share with them, they see me depending on God as I deal with the everyday hassles of life.[8]

Recently I had the pleasure of interviewing one of my favorite people, Chuck Swindoll. Chuck is the president of Dallas Theological Seminary, the master teacher on the syndicated "Insight for Living" radio program, and the baby of his family.

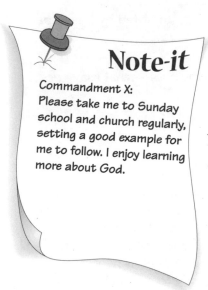

As I was wrapping up our interview, I asked him if he could give other parents and me a tip. He responded almost immediately: "When you don't know, simply say you don't know. Be authentic. Develop an authenticity with your children. Be real."

Be Approachable

Children look up to adults. Adults are so much bigger, and they can do so much more. Adults meet the needs of children throughout the day. It's no wonder little children actually see their fathers and mothers as perfect.

Of course, the mantle of perfection soon drops in tatters from our shoulders. But as long as we have them fooled, we are not doing them any favors with our masquerade. One problem is that when a child sees someone else as perfect, he tends to be uncomfortable. Perfect people are not easy to be around. They don't seem approachable, and if there's anything I want to be as a parent to my children, it is approachable.

Recently I interviewed Rebecca St. James, the Australian Grammy-nominated Christian recording artist. She seemed so mature for her twenty-one years. What had her mom and dad done right? "They were approachable," said Rebecca, eldest of seven children. And because they were approachable, she felt she could talk to her parents about everything. Oh, if we could only have more parents like Mr. and Mrs. St. James!

It is sad to see so many parents refuse—out of pride or selfishness—to let their children know that they do have flaws and that they don't have it all together. When parents are brave enough to share their flaws and lacks with their children, they serve as beautiful models of what it means to depend on God. When you are open and transparent before God and your children, you are saying, "Even though I am many years older, I, too, depend on our heavenly Father, just as I want you to depend on Him."

Another benefit of being open before God and your children is that it motivates them to seek you out and talk about their real feelings. They are more likely to reason, *Mommy won't be mad about this because she had it happen, too.*

Pray with Your Children

One of the best ways to show—not just tell—your children you are truly dependent on God is through prayer. Do you take time to pray regularly with your children? I'm not talking about sitting on your child's bed just before he or she goes to sleep and reciting, "Now I lay me down to sleep. . . ." My children have never heard that kind of prayer. When I pray with them, I pray about the day, about our needs, about specific problems—whatever they might be. We pray for Grandma or Grandpa, for Mom and Dad, or for brother or sister. I pray with them about something we are particularly thankful for that day—a need that was met or an answer that came.

I also pray with our children about my weaknesses and shortcomings. My children do not hear me thanking God for my perfection. They hear me depending on Him for wisdom and strength.

I think prayer time is the most special time of the day for you and your children. I urge you to hold your children as you pray. Take your time, and don't hurry. Stay away from cute prayers and prayers you can memorize. Teach your children to pray from the heart and teach them to pray for their every need.

Allow Godly Freedom

I believe the home should be a place where children can learn to make decisions about their lives and learn to accept the consequences of their decisions—the good and the bad. They need to make choices.

Today's permissive parent takes things a little far. "Brittany, Tyler, McKenzie, it's eight o'clock. Have you *chosen* to go to bed yet? No? You're going to stay up and watch Letterman? Well, okay, Dad and I are going to bed—lock up when you're done." Maybe that's an overdramatization, but you can't always be giving choices to kids. There must be order in the family. Yet some choices are very appropriate, and kids need to be held accountable for their decisions. You can say to little Buford on that cold winter morning, "Would you like Crispy Critters or Cheerios? You decide." Of course he says Crispy Critters. You pour the milk on the Crispy Critters, and what can you assume will happen? Now he wants Cheerios. He has changed his mind. If you retain only one thing, remember this: You can't re-crisp a soggy critter. In other words, once that choice is made, we as parents have an obligation to hold the child accountable for his decision. That's Reality Discipline—freedom and accountability.

The home is really a tuition-free university where children study the lifelong curriculum of decision making. We all must learn how to make our own decisions, including whether or not to accept or reject God's offer of eternal love and salvation. Freedom in Christ is one of the apostle Paul's favorite themes (see Romans 8:21, 2 Corinthians 3:17, and Galatians 5:1). The home ought to be a reflection of God's love. God is in authority over parents but He gives them

> **Note-it**
>
> Godly parenting means treating your children the way God treats us, His children. He lovingly helps us make wise decisions about the realities of life.

freedom and love. Parents are in authority over children, and children also should have freedom and love.

This sounds dangerous to some parents. They keep grasping the concept of control. If they do not control their child, he will get out of hand, he will get hurt, he will go the wrong way. But it's important for us to understand that the tightly controlled child is going to rebel—if not now, then later when he's thirty-two and abandons his family to go and "find himself."

If you stop to think about it, the parent has no other real choice than to give his child freedom. I'm not saying he should neglect his child or let him run into the street and get killed. I'm not saying we should be permissive or authoritarian. Either extreme creates rebellion. At the base of the child-parent relationship should be the parents' desire to train the child, guide him, and set him free to become his own person. The child is becoming an individual anyway. Instead of cramping and crimping the process, you should encourage it and enhance it. That's becoming the parent God wants you to be.

Seeking a Godly Perspective

 Review the four tendencies of Super Parents and how you were tempted. Select the one that troubles you most, and write a prayer asking God to help you release your children to Him. Make it as specific as possible.

Answer key to "Excellence Versus Perfectionism" on pages 20-21: 1 (E); 2 (P); 3 (P); 4 (P); 5 (E); 6 (E); 7 (P); 8 (E); 9 (P); 10 (P); 11 (E); 12 (P); 13 (E); 14 (E)

Portions of this session were adapted from:

Leman, Dr. Kevin. *The New Birth Order Book* (Chapter 5). Grand Rapids, Mich.: Revell, 1998.

Leman, Dr. Kevin. *Bringing Up Kids Without Tearing Them Down* (Chapter 5). Nashville, Tenn.: Nelson, 1995.

Leman, Dr. Kevin. *Getting the Best Out of Your Kids* (Appendix I). Eugene, Ore.: Harvest House, 1992.

Leman, Dr. Kevin. *Making Children Mind Without Losing Yours* (Chapter 5). Grand Rapids, Mich.: Revell, 1984.

For further information, consider:

Leman, Dr. Kevin. *Bringing Up Kids Without Tearing Them Down.* Video series. ©1994 by Dallas Christian Video.

Leman, Dr. Kevin. *Living in a Stepfamily Without Getting Stepped On.* Nashville, Tenn.: Nelson, 1994.

Leman, Dr. Kevin. *When Your Best Is Not Good Enough.* Grand Rapids, Mich.: Revell, 1998.

Leman, Dr. Kevin. *Women Who Try Too Hard—Breaking the Pleaser Habits.* Grand Rapids, Mich.: Revell, 1998.

NOTES

1. Dr. Kevin Leman, *The Birth Order Book* (Grand Rapids, Mich.: Fleming H. Revell, a division of Baker Book House Company, 1985), p. 95. (Dell Mass Market paperback)
2. Adapted from Dr. Kevin Leman, *Making Children Mind Without Losing Yours* (Grand Rapids, Mich.: Fleming H. Revell, a division of Baker Book House Company, 1984), p. 89.
3. Adapted from Dr. Kevin Leman, *Making Children Mind . . .*, p. 90.
4. Leman, pp. 91-93.
5. Dr. Kevin Leman, *Getting the Best Out of Your Kids* (Eugene, Ore.: Harvest House Publishers, 1992), pp. 195-196.
6. Adapted from Dr. Kevin Leman, *Making Children Mind . . .*, pp. 93-94.
7. Leman, pp. 94-96.
8. Leman, p. 103.

PART ONE

Building a Godly Family

"Abel Had It Coming":

The Impact of Birth Order on Family Life

Begin this session by doing a little experiment on birth order that I use in some of my seminars. If you are the facilitator for the session, turn to page 53 in this book for the instructions. Why don't I just spell out the instructions here? Because that would give it away to all the nosy participants in your group who are also reading this page!

And if you're not the facilitator, *don't cheat!*

After the experiment, continue with the following material.

Percy the Perfectionist or Baby Bubba?

To help you understand what birth order is all about, let's take a little quiz. Which of the following lists of personality traits fits you best? (You don't have to be *everything* on the list, but pick the list that has the most items that relate to you.)

   A. perfectionist, reliable, conscientious, list maker, well orga-
      nized, critical, serious, scholarly, don't like surprises

   B. mediator, fewest pictures in the family photo album,
      avoids conflict, independent, extreme loyalty to the peer
      group, many friends, a maverick

   C. manipulator, charming, blames others, shows off, people person, good
      salesperson, precocious, engaging

If you picked list A, it's a good bet you are the firstborn or only child in the family.

If you picked list B, chances are you are a middle child (secondborn of three children or possibly thirdborn of four, and so on). If you related best to list C, it's likely you are the baby in the family, and somebody had to buy this book for you. (Can't resist teasing the babies of the family because I'm one myself. More on that later.)

Notice, in each case I said "good bet" or "chances are." I don't have any supernatural powers when it comes to identifying the birth order of any person, but extensive research and plain old "law of averages" odds are on my side. Just for fun, when conducting family life seminars, I take a quick look around and spot ten people who I believe are firstborn or only children. I go entirely by their physical appearance. These are the folks who look as if they've stepped off the cover of *Glamour* or out of an ad for the *Wall Street Journal*. Every hair is in place, and they are color- coordinated from head to toe. I usually am correct about nine times out of ten.

Some people in the audience suspect they have wandered into a performance by Merlin the Magnificent by mistake, but of course that's not true. There is, however, something to birth order because the odds definitely prove it. It doesn't explain everything about human behavior—no personality test or system can—but it does give us many clues about why people are the way they are.

 As a supplement to this session, view "How to Make Your Child Feel Special" from the videotape *Bringing Up Kids Without Tearing Them Down*, © 1994 by Dallas Christian Video.

As a practicing psychologist, I have used my training and research in birth order as a useful tool in helping parents understand their children as well as themselves and how they are inclined to parent. Birth order information helps Mary understand why her husband, John, is always so upset by what *she* sees as normal childish behavior in their kids, and John gains insight into Mary's laid-back tolerance of this craziness. Birth order helps both Mary and John get a handle on why ten-year-old Buford can go through life oblivious to his open fly and C+ average, while thirteen-year-old sister Hortense has straight As and a good start on an ulcer.[1]

Who Perches Where on the Family Tree?

Before we talk about the impact birth order has on parenting, let's meet a few typical people whose basic qualities have been programmed by their place in their family of origin.

Meet Festus and Fanny Firstborn

I served for several years as assistant dean of students at the University of Arizona and once asked a leading faculty member of the College of Architecture if he had ever paid attention to where the college's faculty members came from as far as birth order was concerned. He gave me a blank stare and said, "I really have to run, Kevin."

It was probably a good six months before he stopped me on campus one day and said, "Say, do you remember that crazy question you asked me about where our architectural faculty came from? I finally decided to take an informal poll and found that almost every one of our faculty is either a firstborn male or the only child in the family."

That was an eye-opener for my friend, but for me it merely confirmed a basic birth order principle[2]: Festus and Fanny Firstborn tend to wind up in "high achievement" professions such as science, medicine, or law. You'll also find Festus and Fanny among accountants, bookkeepers, executive secretaries, engineers, and, in recent years, people whose jobs involve computers. Festus and Fanny Firstborn typically go for anything that takes precision, strong powers of concentration, and dogged mental discipline.

As a rule, Festus and Fanny tend to be more highly motivated to achieve than their younger brothers and sisters. They also tend to be conscientious to the point of being over-responsible.

Meet Matt and Mary Middleborn

If I want to get a rise out of middleborn children at a parenting seminar, all I have to say is, "Family photo album." They laugh, but often a bit sardonically. The typical story reveals two thousand pictures of the firstborn and thirteen of them. Secondborn children in particular seem to fall victim to this strange phenomenon. It is almost as if Mom and Dad suddenly went on welfare and couldn't buy any film, or the camera broke and wasn't fixed until "baby princess" came along.

Then thirteen-year-old Mary Middleborn falls in puppy love for the first time and wants to give her photo to her boyfriend. She goes to her mother and says, "Hey, Mom, are there any pictures of me without *her?*" Mom looks a little chagrined and shakes her head no. So, the new boyfriend gets the photo—carefully trimmed so older sister's armpit barely shows!

Note-it

Firstborn parents give good direction and leadership and usually do well holding their children accountable. On the other hand, their flaw-picking, perfectionistic nature can lead to discouragement, particularly for their firstborn.

Matt and Mary Middleborn tend to display the opposite characteristics of their driven firstborn siblings. They often act as the family mediators and negotiators who avoid conflict. Paradoxically, Matt and Mary are independent and are extremely loyal to their peer group. They are mavericks with many friends. They may leave home first and find their real companionship outside the home because they feel left out of things in their own family.

While Matt and Mary Middleborn's characteristics are not always easy to predict, one factor is constant: As middle children, they always feel the squeeze from above and below. The middleborn theme song could be, "I'm not the oldest! I'm not the youngest! I'm not the only boy (or girl)! I'm just nobody!"

Meet Leman Lastborn

The year is 1952. The scene is a hot, sweat-soaked gymnasium at Williamsville Central High School in western New York. A hard-fought basketball game is in progress and a skinny little eight-year-old kid is out on the floor during a timeout trying to lead cheers. Pinned on his sweater is an image of the team mascot—a billy goat.

The game is as close as the air. The place is packed with screaming fans, but at that moment the fans aren't screaming for their "Billies." They're all laughing at this little kid, who has gotten the cheer completely backward and forgotten what comes next. His big sister, captain of the Williamsville cheerleaders, is dying of embarrassment, but she has to laugh, too, because this little kid is pretty funny.

But is the eight-year-old guy embarrassed? He doesn't seem to mind at all. In fact, he is looking up at the crowd and enjoying the fact that they are all laughing!

I was that little kid—born last in a batch of three. My sister and brother, Sally and Jack, born first and second, were the real lions of the Leman clan. And then came lastborn Kevin, who got the nickname "Cub" when he was eleven days old. The name stuck, and as I became a toddler and a preschooler I instinctively became aware of how to always be "cute little Cubby." A child may have been born last, but he or she has a sixth sense that says, "You don't have to be least!"

Youngest children are typically outgoing charmers and personable manipulators. They are also affectionate, uncomplicated, and sometimes a little absentminded. Their "space cadet" approach to life gets laughs, smiles, and shakes of the head. Lastborns are the most likely to show up at the Sunday school picnic unzipped or unbuttoned in some delicately obvious area. Without doubt, they can be a little different.

It stands to reason then that the family clown or entertainer is likely to be the lastborn. Nobody told me that—

I just naturally assumed the role. I was the Dennis the Menace type. What I wanted was attention. That was my thing in life—getting people to laugh or point or comment.[3]

Lastborns are also good people persons, so they make good salespeople. Have you ever walked onto a used-car lot to be greeted by a guy with a big smile, white shoes, matching white belt, dark blue pants, light blue shirt, and dark blue polka-dot tie? His first words probably were "Well, what would it take to put *you* in *that* car today?"

Note-it

Firstborn parents are more apt to be into control and therefore sometimes end up being hoverers who rob their children of the opportunity to stand on their own and learn from their mistakes.

If you've ever had such an encounter, it's likely you were dealing with the baby of the family. You have to be careful with these guys—they'll sell you your own house and throw in a paint job by the owner![4]

Not Everyone Fits Their Birth Order Profile

Having described the three main categories of birth order, it is important to add that many variables can change the degree to which a person is shaped by his or her birth order. Here are a few:

1. Gender. A laterborn child may experience many of the expectations and influences put on a firstborn if he or she is the first of that gender. "And *this* is our girl [or boy]!" An only girl with older brothers is the "toy princess" who understands men.

2. A five-year gap between children often creates a "start over." The next child experiences a firstborn's environment.

3. Large families can skew the impact on the middle children. However, the firstborn and the "baby" often follow typical patterns.

4. Twins stand out. Who was born first is often a big deal—especially to the firstborn. Intense rivalries often develop, especially when the twins are of the same gender. However, profound companionship also can exist. Twins are well known for creating their own little world, occasionally speaking a language no one else can understand.

5. Unexpected size differences. If firstborn Buford, age twelve, is five feet tall, and his little brother Moose, age eleven, is five feet six and forty-five pounds heavier, don't be surprised if there's a role reversal.

6. Blended families can disrupt the natural expectations for birth order, which can be very unsettling to the children.

Note-it

When middle children become parents, they're good at seeing both sides of parenting issues. Having grown up without undivided attention from Mommy and Daddy, they identify with their own middle child.

7. A critical-eyed parent many times will, in effect, set up a role reversal. That is to say, the firstborn child pays for the parents overly critical flaw-picking eye. The firstborn in this scenario is most likely to become a procrastinator, a person who runs hot

and cold, changes directions frequently in life and never quite measures up to his or her potential. These people as youngsters were the ones you had to push to get them to finish tasks. As adults their desks in the work place have piles all over them. The irony is that if someone asks them to find something in this mess, they could do so most easily. In fact, they know *exactly* what pile to look at. There is order within the disorder.

In other words, the parent's critical eye makes the first child not measure up, so to speak, and not live up to his or her potential, which allows the secondborn to take advantage of the flaw-picking that is done by the parent to the firstborn child. The firstborn is the shock absorber in life for the rest of the family. He or she gets the brunt of it.

8. And finally, each person is unique. God didn't make every person's fingerprints different to help the FBI. While the family situation is profoundly different for each child, we are not the raw products of determinism. Our individual *response* to our environment ultimately declares who we are.

Testing How Some Biblical Characters Fit the Model

One way to see both the common characteristics of birth order and the ways variables can trigger deviations is to look at a group of people we are familiar with. The following list of biblical characters provides such a sample. The birth order of some of these people is not conclusive, but see what you can discover.

 Check off the probable birth order for each person below. Look up the accompanying reference if you are unfamiliar with a person's family life. If necessary, check the answer key on page 52.

	Only Child	First	Middle	Last		Only Child	First	Middle	Last
Aaron (Exodus 2:1-4; 7:7)	□	□	□	□	John the Baptist (Lk. 1:5-13)	□	□	□	□
Abel (Genesis 4:1-2)	□	□	□	□	Joseph (Genesis 37:3)	□	□	□	□
Cain (Genesis 4:1-2)	□	□	□	□	Lazarus (Lk. 10:38-40; Jn. 11:1-5)	□	□	□	□
David (1 Samuel 17:12-14)	□	□	□	□	Martha (Lk. 10:38-40; Jn. 11:1-5)	□	□	□	□
Esau (Genesis 25:19-26)	□	□	□	□	Mary (Lk. 10:38-40; Jn. 11:1-5)	□	□	□	□
Esther (Esther 2:7)	□	□	□	□	Miriam (Exodus 2:1-4; 7:7)	□	□	□	□
Gideon (Judges 6:11; 8:19)	□	□	□	□	Moses (Exodus 2:1-4; 7:7)	□	□	□	□
Isaac (Genesis 21:1-5; 25:1-2)	□	□	□	□	Noah (Genesis 5:28-30)	□	□	□	□
Ishmael (Genesis 16:15–17:5)	□	□	□	□	Samuel (1 Samuel 1:1-11, 20-25)	□	□	□	□
Jacob (Genesis 25:19-26)	□	□	□	□					

Now divide into groups according to your own birth order (combine firstborns and only children if need be). Discuss your biblical counterparts. In which ways were they typical? What factors may have influenced how they varied from their birth order norm?

Why Are We the Way We Are?

What Makes the Firstborn Tick?

There are at least two good reasons firstborns usually come in such downright-upright (and sometimes a little uptight) packages. Those two reasons are *Mom* and *Dad*. Brand new parents tend to be a paradox when it comes to their firstborn child. One side of them is overprotective, anxious, tentative, and inconsistent. The other side can be strict in discipline, demanding, always pushing and encouraging more and better performance.

The simple truth is, the firstborn is a guinea pig as Mom and Dad try to learn the fine art of parenting. After all, they have never done this before. *Everything* about the firstborn child is a big deal, and it starts well before little Festus or Fanny arrives. While Mom is pregnant, the very air is charged with expectancy in more ways than one.

There is little doubt that the family overdoes things with the firstborn. Grandparents always add to the fun by recording every cry, look, whim, or burp on video (or at least on Grandma's old faithful Instamatic).

It's not surprising that research indicates firstborns walk and talk earlier than laterborns. With all the coaching, prodding, and encouragement they get, they probably do it in self-defense! They go on to become the leaders and achievers in life.[5]

It's no wonder firstborns often grow up to be serious, conscientious, and cautious. Mom and Dad have taught them to be wary of life's shoals, reefs, and rocks. At the very least they have learned to pull their oars. How often they hear, "I know your sisters and brothers are acting silly, but they're younger. I expect more from you. You have to be grown up."

When firstborns can't quite hack it with all these expectations, pressures, and demands, they may wind up in a counselor's office. The majority of people who seek counseling help are firstborn or only children. They have tried their best to be conscientious, achieving, dependable, mature—in a word, perfect. The result often is frustration and a great deal of guilt.

I have counseled many firstborn people who feel that they have to walk the line while the rest of the world wanders from one lane to the other without seeming to pay any consequences. It's not quite that way, of course, but when you've grown up carrying the weight of responsibility, character, and values, the load can get heavy indeed.

Firstborns are "first come" and "first served" by eager parents who want to do this job of parenting better than anyone has ever done it before. But in the long run, they are also first into the pressure cooker of life, where they have to produce or else.[6]

Middleborns Just Don't Get Much Respect

While firstborns typically have fewer friends, it is common for middleborn children to have many friends and to hang out more with their peer group than any other child in the family. There is a psychological theory that explains this pattern. It says human beings operate according to three natural motivations:

1. To obtain rewards and recognition

2. To avoid pain and danger

3. To get even

Every birth order has these three motivations operating in life, but it is especially interesting to trace their effect on the behavior of the typical middleborn.

To obtain rewards and recognition, the squeezed-out middleborn goes outside the family to create another kind of "family" where he or she can feel special.

"How sad," you might say, "that the middleborn child has to go outside the family to get recognition and feelings of acceptance." But weep not for our social butterfly. All these relationships will pay off later.

To avoid the pain and frustration of being told "You're too young" when she seeks the same privileges as the oldest, and when weary of hearing "You're too old" when he whines for a little of the TLC given the youngest, the middle child goes to the peer group where he or she is just the right age.

And *to get even* for feeling at least a little bit rootless, the middle child becomes a bit of a free spirit. She gives herself the right to reject the family's do's and dont's, at least in part, by choosing some other group's values as a measuring stick. It may be a team (middle children are great team players), a club, or a gang of kids who hang out together. The important thing is that the middle child experiences the group as his or hers, something the family can't control in any way.

Some middle children choose other ways to meet their needs for obtaining recognition, avoiding pain, and getting even. Because they can't have Mom and

Note-it

Middle children make pretty good parents. They're relational, and they can negotiate well to solve family problems. But sometimes they're too secretive, withholding their true feelings so their children don't know them.

Dad all to themselves and get their way, they learn to negotiate and compromise, preferring to become mediators (and at times manipulators). But these obviously aren't such bad skills to have for getting along in life. (If you are getting the message that middle children just might turn out to be the best-adjusted adults in the family, you're right. More on that later.)

The middle child's propensity to compromise can backfire, however. When an attractive, nicely dressed wife and mother (who is a middleborn) comes to me for counseling, I too often discover this pattern: She's been married for twenty to thirty years and has raised several children. She's been something of a superwife and supermom—and her husband has been having affairs throughout their marriage.[7]

Why has she tolerated this behavior? She is following her basic lifestyle, which taught her to be a pleaser, not wanting to rock the boat and wanting the oceans of life to be as smooth as possible.

True, part of her endurance comes from her love for her husband and her family, but a great part of her motivation is her need to have peace at just about any price —*and her abusive husband knows it.*

Why Lastborns Love the Limelight

There were at least two good reasons for my thirst to achieve "stardom": a brother five years older who scored 9.75 in everything, and a sister eight years older who was a perfect 10. Ever since I can remember, it seemed that I scored around 1.8 in comparison to their abilities and achievements.

But I was determined to get my share of the attention. As a five-year-old, I went to a relative's wedding and became forever established in her memory book when it came time to throw the rice. Everyone else was throwing rice, but Kevin was throwing gravel.

No wonder, then, when I turned eight and my cheerleader sister Sally invited me to become the "mascot" for the high school team that I jumped at the chance. Hundreds of people came to those games, and they all looked right at me! I loved every minute of it, even that embarrassing scene when I forgot the cheer and the crowd roared with laughter. In fact, at that moment, in the Williamsville High School gym, I made a life-changing decision. I decided to be an entertainer.

Yes, I know I turned out to be a psychologist who is practicing family therapy with good results. I enjoy my chosen profession and get deep satisfaction from helping families, but

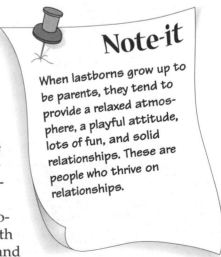

Note-it

When lastborns grow up to be parents, they tend to provide a relaxed atmosphere, a playful attitude, lots of fun, and solid relationships. These are people who thrive on relationships.

my cherished avocation is making people laugh, and I do it whenever and wherever I can—in seminars, at conventions, and during talk shows. Frankly, it's not a bad combination. Humor can be very therapeutic, helping us keep things in perspective.

But there is a negative trait often found in lastborns. Besides being charming, outgoing, affectionate, and uncomplicated, they also can be rebellious, critical, temperamental, spoiled, impatient, and impetuous.

I can relate to this "dark side" of the lastborn. Without question, part of my motivation for being clown prince of the Leman family was that I wasn't born *crown* prince or princess. Sally and Jack had beaten me to it. It seemed to me they had all the talent, ability, and smarts. They had all the firepower, and I was a dud.

Lastborns typically have a burning desire to make an important contribution to the world. From the time they are old enough to start figuring things out, they are acutely aware they are youngest, smallest, weakest, and least equipped to cope with life. After all, who can trust little Leman to set the table or pour the milk? He's just not quite big enough for that yet.

The lastborn's early achievements (tying shoes, learning to read, telling time, and so on) are often greeted with polite yawns and murmurs of "Isn't that nice" or worse: "Horace, do you remember when Festus learned to do that?" Festus, of course, is the big brother, born first.

Lastborns instinctively know that their accomplishments carry far less weight than do those of their older brothers and sisters. Not only do parents react with less spontaneous joy at the accomplishments of the lastborn, they may, in fact, impatiently wonder, *Why can't this kid catch on faster? His older brother had this down cold by the time he was two and a half.*

Part of the reason for this is that parents get all "taught out" by the time the lastborn arrives. The tendency is to let the lastborn shift for himself. It's no wonder the lastborn grows up with an "I'll show them!" attitude, dreaming up new ways to get attention.[8]

However, growing up the youngest can turn one into a bundle of ambivalence. Clownish or manipulative behavior gets a lot of attention, but often at a high price to one's self-image. Therefore, lastborns are on a seesaw of emotions and experiences that they find hard to explain or understand. We can be charming and endearing one minute, rebellious and hard to deal with the next. We can turn from powerhouses of energy into basket cases who feel helpless. We can feel on top of the world on Monday and at the bottom of the pile on Tuesday.

Sizing Up Your Own Flock

You had no say in where you landed in the birth order in your family, and neither did your children. Birth order "happens." But each branch on the family tree has both strengths and weaknesses, advantages and disadvantages. It gets complicated (or more interesting!) when you mix your own birth order tendencies with the birth order tendencies of your children. This is called "parenting."

Reality Discipline involves the process of helping your children maximize their positive tendencies and manage their negative tendencies in a healthy way. We'll focus on that more specifically in session 7, "Birth Order and Parenting: Should You Treat All Your Children the Same?" (Of course, it *is* possible to mess it up like Isaac and Rebecca in the Bible, who not only treated their children differently but played favorites and used their children's tendencies for selfish ends. The good news is that God redeemed that situation—but I'm digressing.)

In the meantime, why don't you review your own family and where you perch on the family tree, then size up your own flock of little buzzards.

 Working individually, answer the following questions[9] that characterize the family in which you grew up and how it affected you.

- What is your birth order: Only child, firstborn, middle child, or baby of the family?

- As you were growing up, what was the atmosphere in your family: cold and hostile; warm, friendly, supportive; neutral, neither warm nor cold?

- Pick the parent who has the most influence in your life and write some words or phrases to describe that parent.

■ Now focus on the other parent and put down words or phrases to describe him or her.

■ Describe yourself between the ages of five and twelve years old.

■ Jot down two or three of your earliest childhood memories (preferably before the age of five or six). Note the emotions present in the memory (were you happy, sad, angry, and so on?).

Go back over your answers to see if you can find any telltale words or phrases that give you clues about how you parent your own children today. Pay particular attention to the way you have described your parents.

Now, in the left-hand column list your children by birth order and jot down their personality traits. (If you have more than three children, use a separate sheet of paper.) In the second column, list any variables that might affect birth order (middle child but first girl, five-year gap in age, and so on). In the third column, jot down how you tend to relate to each of your children (always at odds? easygoing? impatient? frustrated? think alike? drive you crazy? opposites? kindred spirits?).

Firstborn's name: _____

Words describing firstborn:	Variables for firstborn:	How I relate to firstborn:

Middleborn's name: _____

Words describing middleborn:	Variables for middleborn:	How I relate to middleborn:

Lastborn's name: _____

Words describing lastborn:	Variables for lastborn:	How I relate to lastborn:

> Compare your lists with those of your spouse or a close friend. Do you see your children differently? Similarly? In what way do you think the birth order of you and your spouse accounts for the differences or similarities you see? Talk about your preferred ways of parenting. How do your differences and similarities relate to your birth order? How important do you think it is to be on the same page with your spouse?

Suppose you want to change the ways in which you relate to your children. Can it be done? Or are you doomed to say, "Oh, no, I said I'd never parent my children that way, and here I am trapped in patterns I learned from my own parents."

First, the bad news: The grain of your wood is set. Your basic lifestyle was determined long ago. Your birth order had much to do with your choice of certain roles you play in life. And your childhood memories confirm the lifestyle you chose and your perceptions of your world.

But the good news is that you *can* change your behavior. You can know yourself well enough to be able to recognize what you are doing to your children and stop it. You don't have to blow to and fro between the winds of authoritarianism and permissiveness. You can learn to be firm but fair, in loving authority over your child, in control but not a controller, with flexible rules, not rigid ones.[10]

 With your spouse or a close friend, select one of your tendencies that you would like to change. What will you have to do to behave differently?

 Pray now for the power to accomplish some change, and then set a time during the week when you will check in with each other on how it is going, and continue your prayer for one another.

Answer key for biblical character exercise on page 44:

	Only Child	First	Middle	Last
Aaron (Exodus 2:1-4; 7:7)			✓	
Abel (Genesis 4:1-2)			✓	
Cain (Genesis 4:1-2)		✓		
David (1 Samuel 17:12-14)				✓
Esau (Genesis 25:19-26)		✓		
Esther (Esther 2:7)[11]	✓			
Gideon (Judges 6:11; 8:19)		✓		
Isaac (Genesis 21:1-5; 25:1-2)			✓	
Ishmael (Genesis 16:15–17:5)		✓		
Jacob (Genesis 25:19-26)			✓	
John the Baptist (Luke 1:5-13)	✓			
Joseph (Genesis 37:3)[12]				✓
Lazarus (Luke 10:38-40; John 11:1-5)[13]				✓
Martha (Luke 10:38-40; John 11:1-5)[13]		✓		
Mary (Luke 10:38-40; John 11:1-5)[13]			✓	
Miriam (Exodus 2:1-4; 7:7)		✓		
Moses (Exodus 2:1-4; 7:7)				✓
Noah (Genesis 5:28-30)		✓		
Samuel (1 Sam. 1:1-11,20-25; 2:21)[14]		✓		

Opening Exercise for Session 2

If you're the facilitator of a large group doing this course, hold this page up to a mirror and follow the instructions.

Ask participants to divide themselves up into mini-groups according to their birth order: firstborns in this corner; only children in that one; middle borns in another corner; last borns in another. Tell them to arrange their chairs in a circle. While they're getting themselves arranged, walk around the room and unobtrusively place a piece of paper face down on the center of the floor in each mini-group. On the side of the paper facing the floor you will have written this message (not backwards, of course):

Congratulations!

You are the leader of this group. Please introduce yourself to the others in your group and then have each person do the same. As you talk together, make a list of the personality characteristics that you all seem to share. Be prepared to report back to the rest of the seminar with your "composite picture" of yourselves. Please start to work immediately.

Once you've left the paper on the floor, don't do anything else. Answer no questions. Leave the room if you want to. After ten minutes, return and ask if the reports are ready. Note the responses of the different groups. Did someone in the firstborns or only children groups take the initiative and pick up the paper? What about the middle and last borns? Most likely they were so busy in chitchatting that they ignored the paper.

Portions of this session were adapted from:
Leman, Dr. Kevin. *The New Birth Order Book* (chapters 1, 3, 6, 7). Grand Rapids, Mich.: Revell, 1998.
Leman, Dr. Kevin. *Bringing Up Kids Without Tearing Them Down.* Video series. © 1994 by Dallas Christian Video.

For further information, consider:

Leman, Dr. Kevin. *Bringing Up Kids Without Tearing Them Down*. Nashville, Tenn.: Nelson, 1995.

Leman, Dr. Kevin. *Keeping Your Family Together*. New York: Dell, 1992.

Leman, Dr. Kevin. *The Pleasers: Women Who Can't Say No—and the Men Who Control Them*. Grand Rapids, Mich.: Revell, 1987.

NOTES

1. Adapted from Dr. Kevin Leman, *The Birth Order Book* (Grand Rapids, Mich.: Fleming H. Revell, a division of Baker Book House Company, 1985), pp. 14-16 (Dell Mass Market paperback).
2. Leman, p. 17.
3. Leman, pp. 131-132.
4. Leman, p. 147.
5. Leman, pp. 62-63.
6. Leman, pp. 74-75.
7. Leman, pp. 122-123.
8. Leman, pp. 132-136.
9. Dr. Kevin, Leman, *Bringing Up Kids Without Tearing Them Down* (Nashville, Tenn.: Thomas Nelson Publishers, 1995), p. 49.
10. Adapted from *Bringing Up Kids . . .*, p. 47.
11. While it is uncertain whether Mordecai had any other children, it is probable that the orphan, Esther, was an only child since Mordecai is not said to have adopted any other siblings.
12. While Jacob had another son, Benjamin, even younger than Joseph, during the time of Joseph's life in the home, he was definitely the "baby."
13. There is no conclusive evidence that Martha was the oldest, Mary the middle child, and Lazarus the lastborn, but several things about the way they are introduced (especially their home being described as Martha's home) suggest this order.
14. When Samuel was weaned is uncertain, but he probably was old enough not to require infant care from Eli—possibly four or five. That would have given him some experience as the "baby" in the larger household.

Attila the Hun or Milton Milktoast:

Isn't There a Better Way to Parent?

How often at the park, nursery school, or grocery story have you witnessed children practicing the tactics of domestic terrorism even before they can repeat the alphabet? The parent's end of the conversation usually goes something like this: "It's time to go now, Buford. . . . Yes, you do have to put on your snow pants—hold still!—because it's really cold outside. . . . P-l-e-a-s-e stop kicking Mommy! . . . If you don't come now, I'm going to leave you. . . . Guess you'll have to stay at nursery school all night . . . in the dark . . . by yourself. Mommy's going now. Bye! I'm leaving. . . . Okay, we'll stay five minutes more, but only five."

Right! At that rate, they'll be lucky to get home by midnight and probably not before Mommy has walloped Buford so hard he's got her on child abuse charges.

What would you do? What is your style for handling the normal childhood occupation of testing boundaries? Every parenting style really boils down to one question: *How do you use your parental authority?*

Yes, parents do have authority over their kids. Authority is clearly implied in being a parent. The word *parent* means source, progenitor, guardian, and protector. The question is not, *Do you have any authority?* The real questions are: *Do you use your authority in a nurturing and effective way? Is your style of parenting constructive or destructive?*

To get an idea of what kind of parenting style you tend to use, check how the following statements reflect your response when your children require discipline.

IN YOUR OPINION . . .

	Usually	Sometimes	Seldom	
1. When in the company of adults, children are to be seen and not heard.	☐	☐	☐	___ 1
2. Children have just as much right to express themselves as adults do.	☐	☐	☐	___ 2
3. When there is misbehavior, I try to ask questions before responding.	☐	☐	☐	___ 3
4. To "reduce" a consequence would undermine my authority.	☐	☐	☐	___ 4
5. To get my kids' attention, I must raise my voice.	☐	☐	☐	___ 5
6. I will listen to my kids if they want me to change some of the family rules.	☐	☐	☐	___ 6
7. It's important for my children to obey me completely the first time I speak.	☐	☐	☐	___ 7
8. I don't believe other people have the right to correct my kids.	☐	☐	☐	___ 8
9. I seek my children's opinion on as many matters as possible, depending on their age.	☐	☐	☐	___ 9
10. Kids' explanations are just excuses for not obeying.	☐	☐	☐	___ 10
11. If no one is being hurt, I don't challenge my kids on their behavior.	☐	☐	☐	___ 11
12. My children know that they can question me if they think I am being unjust.	☐	☐	☐	___ 12
13. When it comes to my children, my opinion is right most of the time.	☐	☐	☐	___ 13
14. I have few expectations for my kids.	☐	☐	☐	___ 14
15. I make sure I am available to listen to my children's problems.	☐	☐	☐	___ 15

In the margin to the right of each question, place a 3 for every "Usually" checked, a 2 for every "Sometimes" checked, and a 1 for every "Seldom" checked. Then tabulate your scores as follows:

Add the scores from 1, 4, 7, 10, 13 ___   (Authoritarian)
Add the scores from 2, 5, 8, 11, 14 ___   (Permissive)
Add the scores from 3, 6, 9, 12, 15 ___   (Authoritative)

Your highest total may suggest your *tendency* in parenting styles. This does not prove anything because many factors could have influenced how you answered the questions, but it may be a starting point in considering your parenting style.

As a supplement to this session, view "The Three Basic Types of Parents" from *Bringing Up Kids Without Tearing Them Down,* © 1994 by Dallas Christian Video.

The Three Basic Types of Parenting

In the course of my counseling work, I have identified three basic types of parenting, with variations. They are the *authoritarian* style, the *permissive* style, and what I call the *authoritative* style. In brief, they are characterized as follows:

Authoritarian—Discipline is strong-armed, allows no argument, and the parent remains in total control. Everyone knows his or her place and stays in it. However, children raised by authoritarian parents often grow up to be passive, lacking drive, creativity, and initiative; however, sooner or later they tend to rebel—to the total consternation of their parents. Authoritarianism produces rebellion because it tends to

- tell kids they don't count and aren't important, a concept that at some point they will reject unless they have been crushed.
- raise barriers by setting up an "us versus them" mentality.
- make bonding difficult.
- squelch feelings and ideas.
- batter self-image until children are content to be followers and can't stand on their own against temptation.
- produce a warped view of God as an authoritarian.
- discourage (or not permit, in some cases) asking questions.

Permissive—Permissiveness is propelled by guilt. Parents want to be their child's best buddy, all hung up on love, love, love. Permissiveness produces rebellion because it tends to

- tell kids they have a right to unearned rewards.
- tell them they are "equal" to parents.
- treat them (rather than God) as the center of the universe.
- cultivate takers rather than givers.
- teach them to look at everything in terms of "What's in it for me?"
- provide few guidelines and limits.

Authoritative—These parents do not stir up anger in their children. Instead, they bring them up in the training and instruction of the Lord. This style does not produce rebellion because it

- develops consistent, loving limits.

Attila the Hun or Milton Milktoast: Isn't There a Better Way to Parent? 57

- provides the child with decision-making opportunities.
- holds the child accountable.
- lets reality be the teacher.
- conveys respect and love that enhance self-esteem.
- emphasizes communication between parent and child.
- stresses the relationship between parent and child rather than just a set of rules.

 Divide into groups of about four people each, trying to keep couples together. Have each person read one of the following passages and then summarize it for the others.

A. Eli and his sons—1 Samuel 2:12-17,22-30

B. Joseph and Mary with Jesus—Luke 2:39-52

C. Laban and his daughters—Genesis 29:14-30;31:3-7,14-16,22-31,38-42

 Now, working as a team, match each of the following statements to one family, indicating with an A for Eli, B for Mary and Joseph, or C for Laban.

What Three Biblical Families Teach Us

___ Allows children to think they are "entitled to . . ."

___ Controls everything (even for the kids' "good")

___ Gives children freedom within safe bounds

___ Lets children think they are the center of the universe

___ Treats children like property

___ Leads children to God

___ Threatens force to maintain control

___ Allows gross misbehavior

___ Respects children's ideas

___ Tolerates violence and bullying behavior

___ Manipulates children's environment

___ Permits disrespect of others

___ Does not let children go

___ Recognizes rites of passage (letting kids grow up)

 In your own words, briefly describe how the children of each parent turned out.

Mary and Joseph:

Eli:

Laban:

Reconvene as a whole group, and review the following information. (See the Introduction on pages 13-16 for options or ideas on how to do this.)

Both Eli's and Laban's children embarked on serious rebellion. Eli's sons engaged in severe wickedness, and even Laban's children turned against him. Note in Genesis 31:15-16 how his daughters say, so to speak, "Forget him. He's never done anything for us." And this was after Laban went to great pains to make sure Leah got a husband. You would think that she, at least, would be grateful, but no child cherishes that kind of control in her life. Rachel was so resentful of her father that she stole some of his prized possessions, his family idols.

Eli's family, which we might label permissive, and Laban's family, which we might label authoritarian, *both* produced rebellion in the children.

How would you characterize Jesus' behavior at age twelve? He goes off on His own without telling—let alone asking—His parents. When they find Him, He says, "Why were you searching for me? . . . Didn't you know I had to be in my Father's house?" (Luke 2:49).

An authoritarian parent would have said, "Don't you ever speak to me like that again, Bud, or I'll apply the board of education to the seat of understanding. Are we clear on that?" Instead, Jesus' mother "treasured all these things in her heart" (verse 51). Why? Was it that something greater was going on that exempted wise parenting responses? Or were her and Joseph's responses part of the godly parenting needed by Jesus? Notice that the whole event is introduced with "And the child grew and became strong; he was filled with wisdom, and the grace of God was upon him" (verse 40) and ends by telling us that "Jesus grew in wisdom and stature, and in favor with God and men" (verse 52).

Authoritarianism Has Been Around a Long Time

Laban didn't start anything new when he treated his girls like property, pulled Jacob into his net, and threatened force to retain control. The authoritarian approach to parenting has been around ever since the first caveman waved his club at his kids and said, "As long as you live in this cave, you'll do things my way or I'll throw you to the saber-toothed tigers."

Today, of course, authoritarian parents have become a bit more sophisticated, but the basic attitude is the same. Children raised by authoritarian parents get distinct messages: "Obey or else." "Don't talk back." "Children should be seen but not heard." "As long as you live under my roof, you'll do it because I say so, and that's that!"

Authoritarian parents love the motto "Spare the rod and spoil the child," which they mistakenly believe comes from the Old Testament. The Old Testament does talk about the rod, but the actual text of the verse says: "He who spares the rod hates his son, but he who loves him is careful to discipline him" (Proverbs 13:24).[1] The word I love is "careful." It's my conviction that when King Solomon used the word "rod," he meant it as a means of loving correction and guidance rather than just as a tool to inflict pain. Why else would Solomon's father, King David, write, "I will fear no evil . . . your rod and your staff, they comfort me" (Psalm 23:4)? Obviously, there was no fear that the rod would be laid across his back if he happened to make a wrong turn in the path.

Am I saying there is never a time for an appropriate spanking? No (we'll discuss that in session 10). But authoritarian parents who apply the spare-the-rod philosophy to every situation are people who, like Laban, desperately need to control their children. Authoritarian parents demand obedience—as instantly as possible. Questioning, asking "Why?" and, heaven forbid, disobeying the rules are grounds for swift and often severe punishment. If children try to explain what happened, they are considered "mouthy and disrespectful."

Authoritarian parents don't believe in wasting time with dialogue. It is a bit of an understatement to say that, in the authoritarian home, verbal give-and-take is not encouraged. Not only is verbal give-and-take discouraged, it is not even considered an option.

Have you ever tried to greet a dog only to have it cower on the floor? What does that tell you about how that pet has been treated? Some people are like that. They put themselves down before others get the chance. Sometimes such self-protection is the response of someone who has experienced harsh, authoritarian treatment.

All authoritarian parents share one basic characteristic: *they always expect to be in complete control of those under their authority.* Being in control means making all the decisions. As when Laban tricked Jacob into marrying Leah, authoritarian parents are absolutely sure they know best and set out to bring it about. They are strong on control but weak in love and compassion.

One reason authoritarianism appeals to some parents is that it seems to work— for a while. In fact, it may seem to work through most of a child's growing-up years. But make no mistake; children raised by authoritarian parents are keeping score and biding their time. Someday, in one way or another, they will have their shot and let their parents know that underneath the facade of obedience they are angry, hurt human beings who are "mad as hell and not going to take it anymore."[2]

All too often the avenue they choose to express their anger has tragic consequences. I have counseled more than one pregnant teenager whose pregnancy was her act of rebellion. Some extend their rebellion well into their thirties, when they have children of their own. They are the ones who are still trying to find out who they really are.

Permissiveness Leads Straight to Rebellion

Authoritarianism used to be considered the old-fashioned, Victorian approach to raising children (or relating to anyone with less power). However, in recent years, it has enjoyed a resurgence among many parents who have become sick and tired of the other extreme in parenting style: permissiveness.

While authoritarian parents are absolutely sure they know best, permissive parents have convinced themselves that they have no idea what's best. Then they feel so guilty about not knowing where to draw the line that all they can do is respond with love, love, love. They are devoted to meeting every need of their little ankle-biters at every stage of life. Permissiveness is unconditional love gone to seed. Not surprisingly, the permissive parent is strong on giving loving support but very weak on control.

Bywords in the permissive home are often such statements as "Whatever you want, honey." "Well, I guess you can stay up and watch the movie—just this once." "I guess you do need the car more than I do—I'll catch the bus." "Yes, I know it's hard to get up—I'll take you to school. It's not that far out of my way." "It's 8 P.M. have you *chosen* to go to bed yet?"

Obvious in these statements are many attempts on the part of the parent to feel noble or to assuage his or her own guilt. After all, if you want to stay up and enjoy the movie yourself, why deny your child the same privilege, particularly if the film is a wholesome one? And isn't letting your teenager use your car while you take the bus a splendid example of self-sacrifice while meeting your child's every need, which, of course, is your mission in life? And, of course, it's a noble mom or dad who can understand why it's hard to get up and who is always able to "be there" to bail out the child.

Permissive parents are always eager to snowplow the roads of life for their children: do their homework for them, get them a job or a position on the team, make sure they are not fired. We are not told exactly how Eli's sons, Hophni and Phinehas, came by their jobs as priests, but "Papa" undoubtedly played a part. Though the boys were in the priestly line of Aaron, we read that Eli "failed to restrain them" (1 Samuel 3:13), suggesting that he at least had authority over his sons' conduct and possibly their installation from the outset, but he did not exercise that authority. This is the classic behavior of a permissive parent.[3]

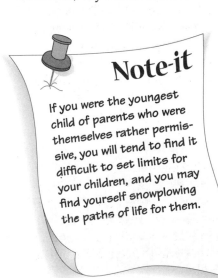

Note-it

If you were the youngest child of parents who were themselves rather permissive, you will tend to find it difficult to set limits for your children, and you may find yourself snowplowing the paths of life for them.

In tolerating his sons' wicked behavior, Eli taught them that they were the center of the universe, not only more important than other people (those who came to make sacrifices), but also more important than God Himself—"they had no regard for the LORD" (1 Samuel 2:12).

Eli finally confronted his sons and whined, "Why do you do such things?" (verse 23), as though they would provide a rational answer. This was the classic bewildered parent: "We don't understand how he (or she) could have done this. We gave him everything he ever wanted!" There is no sadder sight than permissive parents trying to reason with spoiled brats who know they are in control and whose parents are at their mercy. As attractive as permissiveness can look with its seeming nobility and sacrificial aspects, it starts backfiring very early. Eli's sons were full-grown men, but, according to my experience as a counselor, they were probably behaving in much the same way at two or three years of age. I have seen it again and again: Permissiveness leads straight to rebellion. The Bible says Eli's sons "did not listen to their father's rebuke" (verse 25), and you know what vulgar gesture would accompany their response today, because that's exactly the kind of crude adults the Bible says they had become.

Parents come to me wondering, "How can little Percival treat us this way? We've given him everything."

Exactly. And because Percival has had everything, he wants still more. There may be some child-rearing specialists who believe that children are basically good, but I am not among them. Yes, children are cute, sweet, and lovable, but they are also basically greedy and self-centered until they are nurtured, trained, and lovingly disciplined. To bring up a child and not meet his or her needs for nurture and training is to create a little Frankenstein who controls the entire family. In a home with permissive parents, children have the authority, and the parents are the servants. Just watch what happens when the parent tries to say no to something. The routine is always the same. The parent says no, the child cries, and the parent gives in. I know of one case in which a twelve-year-old girl who loved horses whined and complained so much about not being able to have her own horse that her parents moved seventeen miles farther from the father's employment to buy a home with property zoned for horses. That twelve-year-old got her way. Today she is thirty-four years old, single, unusually fond of horses, but so emotionally distant from people that she needs therapy.

The Middle Ground: Authoritative

We've talked quite a bit about the extremes of authoritarian and permissive parenting. We know instinctively and through countless examples and statistical research that neither extreme works very well. That doesn't mean a little dab of each will do the job either. What many parents seem to do is wander inconsistently between the two—permissive to a point, then cracking down with authoritarian wrath. That's like putting one foot in a bucket of hot water and the other in a bucket of ice and wondering why the average isn't comfortable.

I see a lot of parents in this bind. They dangle their child on a yo-yo of inconsistency, then wonder why the kid often acts like a yo-yo.

So, what can parents do? How do you stop the inconsistent swing between authoritarianism and permissiveness? How do you find a middle ground that makes sense to you—and to your child? There are a number of names for that middle ground, but the one I like best is *authoritative*. Don't confuse *authoritative* with *authoritarian*. There is a world of difference. Maybe we should call it *lovingly authoritative* just to make the difference clear. Authoritative parents do not dominate their children or make all the decisions for them. Instead, they use the principles of Reality Discipline, which are tailor-made to give children the loving correction and training of which the Lord approves (Ephesians 6:4).[4]

It is common to identify the authoritarian approach with the law and the permissive approach with grace, but if we know the Scriptures and how God works with us as His children, we also know that *both* law and grace are part of God's plan. As Paul says in Galatians 3:24, "The law was put in charge to lead us to Christ." The law provided the standard, the guideline, the family rules, as it were. Without it we would face chaos, and families are no different. Some people think grace means the elimination of the law. No. Grace is the means of dealing with our violations, our falling short of the law's requirements. And from the beginning, God knew a way of redemption was needed for times when we blew it. That's grace.

 How do law and grace operate in your family? Take a moment to consider your responses as you answer these questions.

■ Does your family have rules that are appropriate for the ages of your children?

■ Are those rules clearly established and not fickle or according to your whims?

■ When the rules are broken, how do you respond? Do you overlook the rule, do you ask questions before responding, or do you swiftly invoke the punishment?

■ Do you seek to allow the situation to teach your child? How does that work?

How can you let the situation teach your child? Well, suppose your seven-year-old breaks a toy belonging to another child. What should you do? What type of discipline is needed in this situation? I believe the discipline ought to be based on *reality*. The reality of this situation is that if you break someone else's property, you apologize and pay for it.

Now, you may be thinking, *Dr. Kevin Leman must be kidding. A seven-year-old kid pay for a toy?* No, I'm not kidding. Your seven-year-old can come up with the money. It comes out of his or her allowance or bank account. (You'd be amazed how many children have bank accounts, usually set up by grandmas and grandpas.)

So, if your seven-year-old breaks another child's toy, you can lovingly discipline him or her by requiring accountability. The child soon learns that this type of behavior—even if it was an accident—costs money, and that's reality.

Of course, you could excuse her for not "intending" to break the toy and pay for it yourself (the permissive response). From this she might learn several things depending on the child's personality or your overtones: (1) What I do doesn't matter, therefore I must not matter. (2) Hey, I can break anything or hurt anyone; someone else will pick up the pieces. (3) I must be no good because I cause other people so much trouble and grief.

Note-it

There is a middle ground that is sane, healthy, and above all, effective. I believe that this middle ground is Reality Discipline, which I define as a consistent, decisive, and respectful way for parents to love and discipline their children.

Or you could give him a good, hard spanking or scream at him, demean him, call him names, and send him to his room (the authoritarian response). These would be what I call punishment. Punishment centers in on the child and misses the real problem. When we punish a child, it is easy for the child to assume that we don't like or love him or her. But with Reality Discipline, you can hold the child accountable for what he or she has chosen to do as you teach the consequences of making a poor decision.

And so, in our own home, when one of our children breaks a toy, it doesn't matter whether it belongs to him or her or to someone else. We do not run out and buy another one to replace it. That would simply teach the child to be irresponsible. Our children would soon get the idea they could break or tear up anything they wanted to and there would always be someone there to replace it for them. That's not realistic, not the way life works. Good discipline is always based on the reality of the situation. And in this case, reality says, "You broke the toy; you pay for another one out of your allowance or (if it belongs to the child) do without."

In session 10, I will expand on how to use the allowance as a teaching and disciplinary tool, and it's amazing how all this works. In so many situations, reality will teach only if you stand back and allow reality to happen.[5]

When we understand this principle of letting the situation teach our children, we will begin to understand a lot more of how God relates to us. So many times we fear He is going to punish us in an authoritarian manner, or we beg for Him to release us from all the consequences of our behavior as a permissive parent would do. Rather, His approach is to forgive us and maintain the relationship while He gives us His strength and support to walk through the consequences of our foolishness. That's often how we mature and learn best.

I believe that parenting and disciplining children in a lovingly authoritative way involves at least four things:

Discipline by way of action. The discipline should be swift, direct, effective, and as closely tied to the violation of the family rule as possible. An example is what we have just talked about. When a toy is broken, it should be replaced, paid for, or mended.

Maintain the relationship by listening to our children. There is great power in listening, but few of us tap that source of power. It's just too easy not to listen—to our children, to our spouses, to just about anyone. Or, when we do try to hear what they say, we're really not listening at a feeling level, and that means we're really not listening at all. Parents sometimes think that if they acknowledge children's feelings out loud, it will only make them feel worse. Exactly the opposite is what really happens. What is needed is to project yourself into what the children are saying—to put yourself in their shoes, so to speak.

This kind of listening is not easy. But here are some suggestions:

- Pay complete attention to what your children are saying. Stop what you're doing, turn to your child with full eye contact, and listen—not only for the details but for the feelings. Frankly, the details won't always make a lot of sense to your adult logic, but that's not what really matters.
- Try to acknowledge the child's feelings with just a word or two, maybe something like: "Oh" or "Uh-huh" or "I see."
- As you identify your child's feelings, name them out loud so your child knows that you know how he or she feels. You might say something like: "No wonder you're upset. That must have really hurt."
- When appropriate, grant the child's wishes in fantasy, even though you can't do much about the reality of the situation. You might say something like: "Sometimes little sisters can be a real pain. I bet you'd like to put a big padlock on your door to keep her out."

At times, wait for a teachable moment. One mother complained that Reality Discipline didn't work with her son. She'd tried to have young Michael get up to his own alarm clock, but he was still late. Being a carpool mom, the other parents and even the kids complained. It was just easier to nag and prod.

"Haven't you ever just left your son at home and taken the other kids to school?" I asked incredulously.

"Leave him home? Oh, I'd never do that."

"Hey, lady," I said, "unless you are willing to take this kid to the mat, he's going to run you in circles for the rest of your life. You need to look for a teachable moment and make your stand."

At first she hesitated, but within a few weeks she got so flustered that she took the other kids to school without Michael. Guess who was standing, waiting in the carport when she got home? Ten-year-old Michael's teeth were brushed, his hair was combed, and he was appropriately dressed for school. And—funny thing— he was suddenly concerned about . . . "Do you know what time it is?" he screamed at his mom.

Rather than get mad or say, "I told you, young man, that one of these days I was going to leave you home" (which does no good whatsoever, so save your breath) she simply lifted her watch and said, "Yeah, Honey, it's ten after nine."

"Mom, I was supposed to be at school at 8:30."

"Well, if you'd like a ride, hop in. I'd be more than glad to take you down to school."

He got in the car, slammed the door, and immediately tried to pick a fight with her. Mom—schooled as she was in Dr. Kevin Leman psychology—kept her happy face and dropped him off in front of the school with the proverbial, "Have a nice day, Honey."

He slammed the door for the second time and went storming into class. Within three minutes, the loudspeaker announced, "Will Michael please report to the vice principal's office immediately."

What's he want with me? worried Michael as he peeked into the vice principal's lair.

"Michael, get in here," ordered the vice principal. "What time does school start, young man?"

"Eight-thirty," whined Michael.

"What time did you get here this morning?"

"Nine-twenty-five."

You can be sure Michael was back in school the next morning at 8:30, and Mom never had another problem getting him up in time.

What had happened? When Mom took the other kids to school, she went in and had a little chat with the vice principal, who was a little bit like the Maytag repairman—waiting to help any parent who wanted to work *with* the school rather than point fingers at the school. Reality Discipline proceeded from that teachable moment.

Note-it

If you are short of time to spend with your children, you need to carefully plan how you use your weekends, vacations, and holidays. Try hiring others to do certain chores so you can spend that time with the kids.

Give ourselves by walking with them through their troubles. Giving of yourself (not things) to your children is an essential ingredient for effective discipline. Many times parents apologetically ask me, "What do I have to offer my children?" I always respond, "You have yourself."

The simple truth is: Children want us. They want our time. But time is very precious, and most of us seem to run out of it too soon. Isn't it ironic that we often run out of enough time for our children? We somehow think that we can get together with them later. Perhaps we can start to spend more time in a few months or after things settle down at work. Strangely enough, the time never seems to magically appear. As we rush through life, time gets even more precious. And before we know it, our children are into their teenage years and then grown and gone, and we never did get to know them. We tried to discipline them without really knowing who they were.

I frequently hear parents talking about "quality time." I understand what parents mean by that, but in all my years of private practice I've never heard one of my young clients (the children) mention "quality time." All a child knows is that he wants your time and your attention, whether it's to watch him do somersaults and cartwheels or to take him for Pig-Out Pizza. In trying to find time for your children, don't worry about how much "quality" is in it. Give them all the time you can, and the quality will take care of itself. As you give them time, you will get to know them. You will be able to build a base for action-oriented and loving discipline.

In Summary: Never forget that children expect adults to discipline them. If the discipline is loving, it will be geared toward instruction, teaching, guiding, and above all, holding a child accountable for his or her actions.

When a parent only punishes, rather than guides and disciplines, the child does not learn much more than how to avoid the pain or unpleasantness of the punishment. At best, it is a negative learning experience.

But if a parent doesn't discipline a child, that parent invites rebellion. In essence, he or she is giving the child a license to hold the parents in contempt. Children can actually develop hatred toward their parents if the parents don't take a stand and discipline them. But if we take that stand, the payoff is tremendous.[6]

Divide into four groups according to the age of your oldest child or the child with whom you are having the most difficulty right now. Read through the scenario on the next page for your child's age and suggest three authoritarian responses and three permissive responses. Then, by yourself, come up with one possible listening/Reality Discipline response. (Even though techniques for Reality Discipline will be explored more fully in later sessions, thinking along those lines is a creative skill to be practiced.) Share your response with the rest of your group.

Practice Identifying Parenting Styles

Feisty Festus

You are walking down the aisle in the department store when *three-and-a-half-year-old* Festus starts pulling you back the other way. He wants Chewy the Pelican who produces a fish-shaped piece of bubble gum in his pouch every time his mouth is opened. You say no and try to continue, but Festus flops on the floor and begins to howl. You go back and tell him to get up. You grab his hand, and his howls escalate to wails as he breaks free, falls flat on his back, and begins kicking his feet. People are looking around the corners and over the counters to see if you are killing him. You have visions of the Child Protection Service coming to get you with its net.

Homework Helper

Your *nine-year-old* son played outside with his cousins right up until dinner. Your brother and his family are guests for dinner, and after the meal all the guys gather in front of the TV to watch Monday Night Football. At 9:30 P.M., you tell your son that it is time for bed. He says he can't go to bed yet because he has to do his science homework. If he doesn't turn it in tomorrow, he can't go on the field trip Friday. "Please! It won't take very long," he begs. Your policy is that he is supposed to finish all homework before doing other things.

Phone Nag

You are on the phone talking to a friend when your *thirteen-year-old* picks up the extension in her room four or five times in less than five minutes. You have clearly spelled out to her that she is not to interrupt while other people are on the phone. You know that it would have been no hardship for her to come out to the kitchen to wait to see when you had hung up, then go back to her own room and use the special extension that you installed for her a few months ago.

Foolish College Freshman

Your *nineteen-year-old* daughter is a freshman in a private college in another state. She has been dipping into her college fund and spending it unwisely throughout the year. Unfortunately, she now finds herself four hundred dollars short for the next quarter's tuition. She calls home with this sad tale, says she has learned her lesson, and asks for help.

Have some fun! After a little planning among your group members, ad lib your scenario for the rest of the group, first with your most outrageous authoritarian response, then with the wimpiest permissive response, and finally with a fair and reasonable authoritative response.

Testing Some Alternatives

In your same teams, share one rule or situation where you have been having trouble. Select something that comes up often so that you will have the chance to test an alternative in the near future. Ask the group to help you devise a response that is more authoritative and less authoritarian or permissive than you have used in the past.

1. One of my problem areas has been:

2. I have usually responded by doing or saying:

3. The result has typically been:

4. I can now see my approach was too *authoritarian* or *permissive* (circle one).

5. In the coming days I will try to respond more authoritatively by doing or saying:

6. I will introduce and explain this new plan to my kids in this way:

7. The results were (record after trying the new response)

■ The first time:

■ The second time:

■ The third time:

> After you have written down your plan, ask the group to pray that you will find an appropriate way to test it before you meet again for the next session.

Portions of this session were adapted from:
Leman, Dr. Kevin. *Bringing Up Kids Without Tearing Them Down* (chapter 2). Nashville, Tenn.: Nelson, 1995.
Leman, Dr. Kevin. *Making Children Mind Without Losing Yours* (chapter 1). Grand Rapids, Mich.: Revell, 1984.

For further information, consider:
Langston, Teresa A. *Parenting Without Pressure.* Colorado Springs, Colo.: NavPress, 1994.
Kageler, Len. *Teen Shaping.* Grand Rapids, Mich.: Revell, 1990.
Leman, Dr. Kevin. *The New Birth Order Book.* Grand Rapids, Mich.: Fleming H. Revell, a division of Baker Book House Company, 1998.

NOTES

1. Adapted from Dr. Kevin Leman, *Bringing Up Kids Without Tearing Them Down* (Nashville, Tenn.: Thomas Nelson Publishers, 1995), p. 26.
2. Leman, pp. 27-28.
3. Leman, pp. 29-30.
4. Adapted from Dr. Kevin Leman, *Making Children Mind Without Losing Yours* (Grand Rapids, Mich.: Fleming H. Revell, a division of Baker Book House Company, 1984), pp. 26-27.
5. Leman, pp. 27-28.
6. Leman, pp. 29-30.

How to Be in Healthy Authority over Your Children

Remember the scene from *The Sound of Music* in which Maria is introduced to the von Trapp children? Father blows a whistle, and in come the children, all spit and polish and marching in step. *Click* go the heels as each one, oldest to youngest, is smartly introduced.

Okay, now, admit it. Haven't there been times when you wished *you* had one of those magic whistles?

Many times we parents feel overburdened about how our children are doing. We command, but they don't obey. They do something that embarrasses us in front of all the relatives at Christmas. The "spit and polish" looks more like "slobber and hair dye." Sometimes our anxiety leads to a harsh, authoritarian response, and sometimes it leads to inconsistency and permissiveness. How is one to walk the tightrope of being that loving, authoritative parent?

Face it, friend. As the old baseball cliché goes, "Nobody bats one thousand." That even includes you, the parent, as well as your children.

It's good to have healthy, realistic expectations for your children, but balance those expectations by fully accepting that they will not always meet your standards or desires. In other words, *take things in stride*. I don't mean you should adopt a *laissez-faire* attitude. But I am saying that it probably won't hurt to lighten up a bit.

Now I realize that it's easy for a laid-back baby of the family like me to give such sage advice, but what about the parent who just isn't that relaxed for one reason or another? Maybe you're a firstborn or only child, and you learned to be a little uptight from the cradle. It isn't natural for you to put a relationship ahead of the rules because the rules are very important. Sure, you try to take things in stride, but there is always that little voice whispering in your ear, "Watch out! If you let your kids get away with this or that, you're not teaching them to be *responsible!*"

I have dealt with literally thousands of parents who have felt "I can't let down now. If I do, the whole family will fall apart." If you end up feeling that way, ask yourself one question: "What difference is this going to make seven or ten or fifteen years from today?" If you think about it, growing up is really a trial-and-error affair. Children make lots of errors, and the parents feel it is a trial.

Try to look at the big picture, seeing the good as well as the problems. When you can do that, your authority can be maintained without your having to constantly draw lines in the sand.

 As a supplement to this session, view "How to Be in Healthy Authority over Your Child" from *Bringing Up Kids Without Tearing Them Down,* © 1994 by Dallas Christian Video.

Dr. Kevin Leman's School of Parenting

To help parents see the big picture that meets children's basic psychological needs while maintaining the parents' authority, I often review some guidelines for living together successfully. At our house, we call these rules for a godly family "Dr. Kevin Leman's Magnificent Seven."

1. Pray for your children; teach them on and at your knees.

2. Be firm but fair.

3. Ask—and give—respect.

4. Learn from mistakes (forgive seventy times seven).

5. What you see is what you get.

6. Real love includes limits.

7. Walk—don't just talk—your values.

These are the same rules I advocate for any parent who comes to see me with child-rearing problems. Let's look at them in greater depth.

Rule 1: Pray for Your Children; Teach Them on and at Your Knees

When we sold our home and built a new one just a mile or two away in the *arroyos* of north Tucson, the contractor who oversaw the building of our house was without question a firstborn child. How do I know? One major clue was his meticulous concern over details. One morning I stopped by the job site at 5:30 A.M. because it would be my only chance to look things over before leaving on a trip. To my surprise, there was Gary.

"I can't believe you're here this early," I said in surprise. "The sun's not even up yet."

"Kevin," Gary replied, "it doesn't make much difference if I'm here for a lot of the things that go into your house, but the one thing I have learned is that this is the time I need to be on the spot. This is the day we put in the foundation, and if the foundation isn't right, nothing else is going to be right, either."

Somehow I think there's a parable for families somewhere in Gary's statement. The foundation of every Christian family must be the Lord. When families don't make that foundation their first priority, then everything else will receive too much, or too little, attention.

In writing his second letter to Timothy, Paul notes two elements of this foundation. First, he speaks of his own regular prayer for Timothy "as night and day I constantly remember you in my prayers" (2 Timothy 1:3). Second, he speaks of the early training in the faith that Timothy received from his mother. He wrote, "I have been reminded of your sincere faith, which first lived in your grandmother Lois and in your mother Eunice and, I am persuaded, now lives in you also" (verse 5).

If we were to dramatize these facts, we might see a family where Timothy, from his earliest years, sat at the knee of his believing mother and possibly even grandmother as he learned of God's love and care for him—and learned to pray to his heavenly Father. That instruction continued throughout Timothy's childhood as it took root and grew into a firm and personal faith.

The next scene portrays the apostle Paul praying every day for the young man, Timothy, much in the same fashion as his mother and grandmother undoubtedly did.

How solid is your family's spiritual foundation?

Perform this brief spiritual checkup by checking the comments that apply concerning your own faith and how it is being conveyed to your children.

1. Concerning my own faith in the Lord . . .

_____ My faith is strong, and my sense of God's presence and care is regular.

_____ My faith is strong, but my relationship with God feels distant.
_____ My faith is weak, but I reach out in prayer regularly.
_____ I have trouble believing and have never established a personal relationship with Jesus.
_____ Other:

2. Concerning my children's awareness of my faith . . .

_____ I tell my children how and why I turn to the Lord on a regular basis.
_____ My children hear me praying for them and the needs of our family.
_____ My children observe me worshiping the Lord in ways that reveal my obvious belief and sincerity.
_____ I report on answered prayer.
_____ I report on times of doubt and struggle, and I tell my children when and how those struggles are resolved.
_____ I don't discuss my faith with my children.

3. Concerning instructing my children in the faith . . .

_____ We have some form of devotions with our children in which they learn basic Bible stories and truths and how to pray.
_____ We pray at meals and bedtime, inviting our children to share what they want to ask Jesus about.
_____ We keep some kind of diary of answered family prayer and review it occasionally with our children.
_____ We take our children to Sunday school and church regularly.
_____ We rarely pray together as a family.

 After considering your answers to this brief checkup, commit yourself to improving your family's spiritual foundation in the following way (write it out in the space below):

Rule 2: Be Firm but Fair

This is the cardinal rule on which all the other parenting rules are based. In the last session we talked about the two major errors that bring parents and their children to my office for counseling: *authoritarianism* and *permissiveness*. Authoritarians tell the child: "My way or the highway." Permissive parents say, "Have it your way, honey, and can I drive you anywhere?"

Both of these approaches fail to meet a child's basic psychological needs (listed in the accompanying Note-it). They leave children feeling unloved, insecure, not belonging anywhere, unapproved of, unrecognized—and operating in a dependent, irresponsible way. Both approaches destroy or erode a child's self-image or sense of self-worth. When used to extremes, both approaches lead straight to serious family problems.

Real-life parenting takes an approach in which being firm but fair is a goal that provides a great deal of flexibility—and freedom to fail. Children have freedom to think, ask questions, and disagree with parents. Children have freedom to feel angry, frustrated, sad, afraid, and so on. They have freedom to express their feelings in an appropriate way.

Note-it

Every child needs to:
- Be loved and accepted.
- Be secure and relatively free from threat.
- Belong; feel included.
- Be approved and recognized for what they do.
- Move toward independence, responsibility, and making their own decisions.

Anger, for example, can be a problem, but it does no good to treat children's anger with authoritarian methods: "You will not be angry! That's an order!" Nor does it help to be permissive: "Mommy is sorry she made you mad, but please don't hit the baby with your truck—it isn't his fault."

The firm but fair method acknowledges children's anger—"I can see you are upset"—and then works out a way for the child to express that anger in a nondestructive or nonabusive way: "If you want to scream, you'll just have to do it in your room. When you calm down, you can rejoin the rest of us and we can talk about it."

To be firm but fair is to be flexible, avoiding the extremes of being too rigid or too pliable. Instead, you are willing to listen, understand, and—on occasion—bend a little.

 Divide into groups of three people and have one person read the following situation. Then brainstorm three possible responses. Make one *firm but harsh*, one *indecisive*, and one *firm and fair*.

Eleven-year-old Percy has neglected his regularly assigned chores again—cleaning his room and the dog pen. He is supposed to have these tasks done by Friday night each week, but it is now 8:30 A.M. Saturday and his soccer game starts in half an hour. His mother has discovered his chores aren't done, and she is already running late for an appointment of her own. She tells her husband what happened. Dad calls Percy in and says, "Your room isn't clean and the dog pen is still filthy. These chores were supposed to be done by Friday night."

"But, Dad, there was a really good program on TV, and I just forgot."

"Well, I think you'd better get your room cleaned up and the dog pen, too—right now."

"But, Dad, I'm going to be late for my soccer game. The team needs me. I'm the only goalie we've got!"[1]

■ Response 1, firm but harsh:

■ Response 2, indecisive:

■ Response 3, firm and fair:

 Reconvene the large group and have volunteers share one or two examples in each category.

Remember, being firm but fair leaves the parent in charge but provides a flexible atmosphere in which children can learn from their mistakes without feeling crushed or stifled by authoritarian insensitivity.

Rule 3: Ask—and Give—Respect

Parents often tell me that they want their children to learn to be respectful. Some mothers have sat crying in my office, sniffling the same complaint made famous by Rodney Dangerfield: "Dr. Kevin Leman, I don't get any respect from my children. They act like little savages."

I realize that turning cute little savages into respectful, responsible citizens is no easy task, but it can be done. The key is not to *demand* respect from your children. Respect is a two-way street. In order to gain the respect of your children, you have to treat them with respect. Try applying the Golden Rule of parenting: *Treat your kids as you would want to be treated.*

Authoritarian parents often make their children "toe the mark" by demanding respect, and woe unto the kid who doesn't give it to them. What these parents don't realize is that they are not getting respect, they are receiving only their children's begrudging compliance, which comes out of fear. The children are biding their time, and there will come a day for payback. I deal frequently with families in which the "respectful" child has decided to pay back the parents in dramatic and even devastating ways.

On the other hand, being respectful of your kids doesn't mean you put them in charge. After all, you are the adult, and you are in healthy authority over your kids. Never forget that. You can still be firm in stating your expectations, while at the same time remembering that all the expectations in the world will not do you much good if you act disrespectfully toward your children and treat them like second-class citizens, or worse.[2]

Examine Ephesians 6:4, which says, "Don't make your children angry by the way you treat them" (NLT). In other words, don't do things that are bound to make them angry. Brainstorm in the whole group the kinds of actions, attitudes, and comments that make you angry and *why.*

Things that "punch my buttons"	Why they upset me
1.	
2.	
3.	
4.	
5.	

Turn to someone next to you and go over the following examples of everyday correcting and teaching relative to table manners. Discuss your responses to the accompanying questions.

"Get those hands washed before you come to dinner. They're filthy!"

- What is the child likely to hear?

- Why might a child be angered by this?

- How might this concern be communicated more respectfully?

"Sit up straight, keep your elbows off the table!"

- What is the child likely to hear?

- Why might a child be angered by this?

- How might this concern be communicated more respectfully?

"At the table, children are to be seen and not heard!"

- What is the child likely to hear?

- Why might a child be angered by this?

- How might this concern be communicated more respectfully?

Admittedly, maintaining a balance between being too harsh and being too soft is not always easy—even for psychologists who write books about it. Once, when my daughter Krissy was a teenager, we were kidding around and she crossed a line by calling me a "moron" in front of several of her friends. I promptly scolded her sharply right in front of her friends and let her know "that kind of language isn't necessary, young lady."

After her friends left, Krissy was sitting glumly in her room. By then I had cooled off. She had not shown me respect, but at the same time I had not been respectful of her. I had simply retaliated and used my parental authority to chastise her disrespect for me.

I knocked on her door and went in and told her, "I'm sorry, I shouldn't have yelled at you in front of your friends. Honey, you know I like to kid around, but you went too far."

"Okay, Dad. I'm sorry—it won't happen again."

As I turned to leave, Krissy added, "Uh . . . Dad. . . "

"What is it?"

"Thanks for apologizing. I won't forget."[3]

Rule 4: Learn from Mistakes (Forgive Seventy Times Seven)

The firm but fair family functions by holding children accountable and responsible for their actions. This isn't done punitively with a "we're-watching-you-so-don't-foul-it-up" attitude. Instead, parents are always available to help children learn from their mistakes while carefully balancing the need to be responsible with forgiveness and love. Firm but fair parents point out what is wrong and invoke logical consequences when necessary, but always within a context of loving forgiveness.

> Sixteen-year-old Betsy has had her driver's license for just three weeks. Over the Thanksgiving weekend, as she is hurrying to pick up a friend to do some Christmas shopping, she backs into Grandma's car parked at the far side of the driveway. She barely dents Grandma's fender, but the damage will run at least $150 to $200 minimum, possibly more.
>
> Betsy is mortified. She comes in the house crying, trying to explain what happened. Her parents remain calm. There is no screaming, no threat to take away her license or her keys. As Betsy continues to sob and vow that she'll "never drive again," Dad comes over, puts his arm around her, and says, "Honey, accidents happen. It's just metal. It can be fixed as good as new. Everything's going to be okay."

 Name three failures you have experienced in your life. Then identify what helped you survive the experience and what you learned from your mistake.

And then Dad works out a deal with his daughter. He goes ahead and gets Grandma's car fixed and, because he has a $500 deductible, that means paying for the repairs out of his own pocket. But then he arranges with Betsy to pay him back over the next few months.

To be firm but fair always allows for failure. When children fear failure, they are hampered and become afraid to try, risk, create, grow, and learn. When parents are understanding, they can turn a failure into a good learning situation.[4]

Failure 1:

■ I survived because:

■ From my mistake I learned:

Failure 2:

■ I survived because:

■ From my mistake I learned:

Failure 3:

■ I survived because:

■ From my mistake I learned:

 Divide into small groups and read Matthew 18:21-35. Discuss how some of your adult failures compare to the mistakes your kids make. How can you translate what helped you survive your mistakes into ways you can help your children survive and learn from their mistakes?

Rule 5: What You See Is What You Get

As the baby of a family, I have never been much of a perfectionist. I find real joy in doing all I can to help firstborns (who make up a major portion of my practice) loosen up and quit trying to live flawless lives. And I hope everyone taking this course—particularly firstborn parents—will loosen up, too, because there simply are no flawless parents. We all make mistakes and some of them can be dillies.

I'm still living down the time I cut Holly off at the ankles over something we've both long forgotten. But I'll never forget the fire in her twelve-year-old eyes and what she said: "You ought to read some of your own books!"

I've had more than one tense encounter with Holly, some of which were her responsibility and some of which were mine. But this time, to be honest, her remark took the wind out of my sails—and almost collapsed my mast. A few minutes later, as she was leaving for school, I stopped her, looked her in the eye, and said, "You know, you're right. I *should* read my own books. I was way off base, and I'm sorry. I apologize."

As kids are prone to do, Holly tried to act nonchalant as if nothing had happened. "Oh, that's okay, Dad, see ya," and off she ran for the car. She may have wanted me to believe it was no big deal, but we both knew differently.

The thing that has saved the day for me more than once with Holly, as well as with my other children (not to mention my wife!), is to be transparent and to admit I'm not perfect.[5]

No matter how hard we try, it's easy to slip back into our old patterns. Your lifestyle will get you every time. That's where transparency becomes your powerful ally and tool. Instead of covering over mistakes, own up to them. Then you don't have to cover them up because they're taken care of and the way is cleared for forgiveness.

Being transparent is only one part of the all-important area called *communication*. Unfortunately, the "C word" has been used so much that it has become a worn-out cliché. Nonetheless, to have a functional family, clear and open interaction between parent and child is an absolute necessity. We will look at this a lot more thoroughly in a later session.

 Working alone, think about a time recently when you regretted how you related to one of your children. Answer the following:

■ If you apologized, how did your child respond?

■ If you didn't apologize, what do you think would happen if you said something about it now?

Rule 6: Real Love Includes Limits

It is vitally important for parents to love their children unconditionally, but this isn't always easy. Real love means that we are kind and compassionate, but we are also firm and fair. In fact, we can't have real love for our children without reasonable, healthy limits to guide and nurture them.

Sometimes parents ask, "Aren't limits 'conditions'? How can you set limits if you are trying to love someone unconditionally?" Limits may put conditions on behavior or privileges: "If you want me to listen to you, then you'll have to speak respectfully." Or "When you finish your chores, then we can go to the game." But limits don't put conditions on your love. We must carefully avoid saying or even implying, "If you're good, I'll love you!" Limits help channel love and give it the substance that makes it real and lasting, not artificial and temporary.[6]

 Divide into groups of threes, separating spouses, and study Proverbs 3:11-12, discussing the following questions.

■ What is implied when a parent does not set limits and discipline a child?

■ How does this proverb suggest ways in which we naturally interpret discipline?

■ What might you do to help your children understand that the limits you set reflect your love?

The trick is to invoke limits without making your children feel you don't love them. According to Ross Campbell, author of *How to Really Love Your Child*, some studies show that 93 percent of all teenage children feel that nobody loves or cares for them. Campbell observes that surely more than 7 percent of all parents love and care for their children, but the catch is that their children don't *feel* loved and cared for.

Campbell says, "The love we have in our hearts for our children isn't automatically transferred to them through osmosis. Children don't know we love them simply because we feel love for them. We must communicate our love for our children in order for them to feel secure in it."[7]

Go ahead—say it! To "communicate" suggests words: talking, writing, and so on. I believe, however, that parents, especially parents of young children, actually can communicate love more effectively without words. Every child needs plenty of hugs, holding, cuddling, kissing—what the textbooks call "tactile stimulation." Then follow up with plenty of talk: kindly words, loving words, appreciation, and encouragement. But go easy on the praise because, strange as it may seem, praise usually doesn't help and can even hurt. We'll talk a lot more about that in session 8.

Go ahead—enjoy 'em! Another way to love your children is simply to enjoy them. Enjoy their earliest smiles and laughter—even their drools and spills and accidents. Watching young children explore, particularly from eighteen months to three years, can actually be fun, even though that includes the infamous period called "the terrible twos." Yes, the twos can test any parent, but they don't have to be terrible. Make it a point just to have fun with your kids at any age—though you might have to catch those elusive teens.

Go ahead—hug 'em! Perhaps I can't emphasize enough that your children need to be touched, particularly the boys. Research shows that as badly as children need physical contact, few of them get enough of it. Supposedly preschool girls get the most touching and cuddling. Some studies say they get five times more than preschool boys. Could there possibly be a connection between this and the fact that little boys have six times as many psychiatric problems as little girls?[8]

The connection is obvious. Our society has always taught its males to be nontouchers or non-huggers. As a rule, parents think it's more important to touch and hug girls than boys. After all, little boys are supposed to grow up to be "big strong men" who don't need all this hugging and touching. Not surprisingly, there is a price to be paid for this lack of tactile stimulation, and boys pay it.

One of the basics in teaching children that they are accepted and they belong is the power of touch. Because boys are touched less, they are much more apt to grow

> ## Note-it
>
> Back off and let children do things for themselves, even if they do not always measure up to your standards. It takes an understanding parent to turn a child's failure into a good learning situation.

up having difficulty getting close to people or learning to develop intimacy with others—their wives, for example. Many of the psychiatric problems men develop are connected to feeling alienated—literally "not in touch" with others.

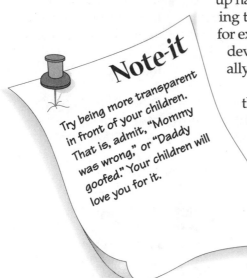

Never underestimate the awesome power of the simple hug. One doctor studied forty-nine different cultures throughout the world to determine what effect physical affection and body touch have on children and adults. He learned that the more violent societies were the ones in which touching and caressing were rare in the family.[9]

I realize that with all of the horror stories coming out today about incest and child abuse, some parents shy away from cuddling and hugging. My only comment is that parents who are predisposed to doing the wrong kind of touching will do it anyway. Healthy parents will do the right kind of touching, and all their kids need plenty of it.

Go ahead—but stop, look, and listen! Along with touching, you can show your love for your children by looking and listening. How often through the day or even through the week do you tune in and focus on your child, looking the child in the eye, and talking lovingly and kindly? And how often do you stop to listen for feelings instead of hurriedly urging the child to give you the facts so you can go on with your busy schedule?

Parents often complain that they can't get their children to tell them what's happening at school or to talk about much of anything. Perhaps a major reason is that, when the children were very small, they were brushed off so frequently they decided that Mom and Dad just weren't that interested. In the godly family, Mom and Dad are always interested, and they let their children know it.

Rule 7: Walk—Don't Just Talk—Your Values

"Woe to you, . . . you hypocrites! You are like whitewashed tombs, which look beautiful on the outside but on the inside are full of dead men's bones and everything unclean. In the same way, on the outside you appear to people as righteous but on the inside you are full of hypocrisy and wickedness" (Matthew 23:27-28). My, my! Such rough language to be coming from our gentle Jesus, meek and mild.

Jesus was addressing the Pharisees, but we parents need to take note, because we, too, are teachers of God's law. There is no more powerful way to teach than by modeling or, more simply, by example. But it cuts both ways!

As parents we fail to realize that how we live each day speaks volumes about what we really value. The choices we make, the words we use, the TV programs we watch, the way we treat others, the way we obey or disobey the law—all are sure-fire communicators of what we think is really important. In one sense, everyone has values; it is only a question of what kind.

> Divide by pairs with spouses or good friends together. Share with the other person one area you think he or she "walks his or her talk"; that is, an area where what the other person believes and teaches is strongly represented by the person's actions. Once you both have identified a positive area in the other person, share an area where you need improvement in living before your children what you believe. Then pray for each other.

- Consistency between my talk and my walk as noted by my spouse or friend:

- The area in my life where I need to improve the consistency between what I say (believe) and what I do:

- One small thing I can do this week to increase this consistency:

Portions of this session were adapted from:
Leman, Dr. Kevin. *Bringing Up Kids Without Tearing Them Down* (chapter 3). Nashville, Tenn.: Nelson, 1995.

For further information, consider:
Glenn, Stephen H., and Nelsen, Jane. *Raising Self-Reliant Children in a Self-Indulgent World*. Rocklin, Calif.: Prima Publishing and Communication, 1989.
Kageler, Len. *Teen Shaping*. Grand Rapids, Mich.: Revell, 1990.
Kesler, Jay, with Beers, Ronald, eds. *Parents and Teenagers*. Wheaton, Ill.: Victor, 1984.

NOTES

1. Adapted from Dr. Kevin Leman, *Bringing Up Kids Without Tearing Them Down* (Nashville, Tenn.: Thomas Nelson Publishers, 1995), pp. 53-55.
2. Leman, pp. 56-57.
3. Leman, pp. 57-58.
4. Leman, pp. 58-59.
5. Leman, pp. 59-60.
6. Leman, pp. 60-61.
7. Ross Campbell, "How Do I Love Thee? Let Me Show the Ways," *Parents and Children*, eds. Jay Kesler, Ron Beers, and LaVonne Neff (Wheaton, Ill.: Victor Books, 1986), p. 545, as quoted in Dr. Kevin Leman, *Bringing Up Kids Without Tearing Them Down*, p. 61.
8. Campbell, p. 546, as quoted in *Bringing Up Kids . . .*, p. 62.
9. Dr. James Prescott's research discussed by Dr. Joyce Brothers, "Childhood Hugs Last a Lifetime," *Los Angeles Times*, Thursday, June 28, 1990, p. E10, as quoted in *Bringing Up Kids . . .*, p. 62.

Do You Have Time to Be a Godly Family?

Maybe you coughed up your life savings for tickets and popcorn and took all the kids to see the movie "Fly Away Home." It's based on the true story of a man named Bill Lishman, who took pity on a batch of day-old Canada goslings that had been orphaned near his Blackstock, Ontario, home. As he tossed them a few kernels of corn, it was one of those "defining moments." The goslings took one look at their two-legged benefactor and decided this funny-looking bird must be "father goose"!

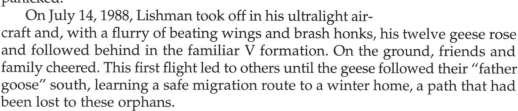

Pretty soon the goslings were following Lishman around everywhere he went. The neighbors probably thought it was cute, but "father goose" had a bigger concern. Young geese need to follow experienced geese the first time they fly south. Who was going to teach these goslings how to follow a safe migration route to their winter home?

Who, indeed? "I became their parent," Lishman realized. "They had imprinted on me."[1] He probably felt the same way I did when I held my beautiful first-born and she looked at me with those big brown eyes of absolute trust. "I don't need to worry," they seemed to say. "Daddy will take care of everything." I nearly panicked.

On July 14, 1988, Lishman took off in his ultralight air-craft and, with a flurry of beating wings and brash honks, his twelve geese rose and followed behind in the familiar V formation. On the ground, friends and family cheered. This first flight led to others until the geese followed their "father goose" south, learning a safe migration route to a winter home, a path that had been lost to these orphans.

As the New Testament so often shows, there's nothing like a good parable. The analogy between Lishman teaching his birds "the way home" and the need for parents to be available to teach their children the same lessons is unmistakable.

Will Your Family Imprint Be Indelible or in Disappearing Ink?

If you're expecting your first child or have children under age seven, this session is especially for you because *there is no more important time in your child's life than now.*

Most parents know, or at least can recall hearing somewhere, that the first five to seven years of a child's life are the most critical in developing the child's personality, character, and emotional makeup. The question is, what part will you play in helping your children develop during those first seven years or so? Is that your main priority, or does your career or some other interest take precedence?[2]

As Lishman illustrates, *someone* will "imprint" your child, showing him or her how to live, how to find the way home, ultimately to our Father's home in heaven—or not. Anyone who lives in a northern city these days has seen the hundreds of geese that have lost their way and spend their winters with nothing to do but hang out on snow-covered corporate lawns, hoping someone will toss them a crumb of bread so they won't starve. Will that be the fate of our children?

Here's a scary thought that Dr. Brenda Hunter points out in her book, *Home By Choice:* The person who teaches your child to talk is the person who teaches your child to think. If your children are in daycare ten to twelve hours a day, that might send a chill or two up any parent's spine. Some say it takes a village to raise a child. For others, it's the neighborhood kiddie kennel. But make no mistake about it: You are the best teacher your child ever will have, and you will do the best job of parenting your child. Staying home might require a great deal of personal sacrifice on your part. But guess what? Look at the generations before us—your mom and dad, their moms and dads. How would you summarize their lives? *Sacrifice* might be an appropriate word.

> Read Deuteronomy 6:6-9. After saying that God's commandments are to be upon *our* hearts, the passage lists eight instructions for passing those values on to children. List them in the column on the left. In the column on the right, suggest contemporary applications.

Biblical Instruction   **Contemporary Application**

1.   1.

2.   2.

3.   3.

4.   4.

Biblical Instruction	Contemporary Application
5.	5.
6.	6.
7.	7.
8.	8.

Go back over your suggestions for contemporary applications and circle those that are made more difficult by your lifestyle. Then divide into groups of four and compare your suggestions, discussing how you can achieve greater influence with your children—including lifestyle changes.

A Window of Time

The Mother Goose/Father Goose image makes sense when you realize you have a limited number of critical moments in your child's life to leave a positive mark. Any basic textbook in psychology usually contains an account of the work of Konrad Lorenz, who is credited with coining the term "imprinting" because of his studies of baby ducks and how they learn to follow their mother. What Lorenz and other psychologists who worked before and after him learned is that the period for a baby duck to learn to follow Mama lasts only about twenty-four hours. According-ing to Lorenz, the imprinting of the baby duck reaches its maximum point at seventeen hours; at twenty to twenty-three hours, the imprinting effect is just about complete.[3]

A study of songbirds by a psychologist named Konishi in the 1960s demonstrated that "song learning in birds is also restricted to a very short period of time and is irreversible. It cannot be repeated later, nor caught up with if that period is missed. Nor can it be changed."[4]

Lorenz and many other psychologists believe there are very real implications in the imprinting concept where humans are concerned. He admits it is a big leap from ducks and songbirds to human infants, but thinks the correlation is there.[5]

I believe Lorenz is right. Obviously, human babies have longer periods for imprinting than ducks. Imprinting, especially

Note-it

While it takes years to build a child's self-image, the first five to seven years are the most important. During that time there are critical moments when you can leave a positive mark. If you aren't there, those opportunities are gone forever.

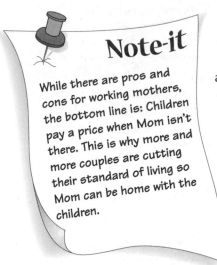

by the mother as she bonds with her baby, goes on throughout infancy, particularly during the first year or so. But if Mom isn't there to do that imprinting, somebody else will. That somebody else is usually a caregiver of some kind.

Research shows that imprinting starts at birth. For example, one study determined that if a mother is with her newborn the first hour following birth and at least five hours in each of the next three days, she is more likely to be an effective parent than one who spent less time with her infant. In fact, this kind of study has shown that when a mother has increased contact with her baby in the first few days and weeks after birth, the baby cries less and grows more rapidly. The mother also has increased affection for her baby and more self-confidence and is much less likely to engage in any child abuse in the immediate years to follow.[6]

On the other hand, if a mother has her baby and goes back to work in the next few days, weeks, or even months, she has less opportunity to bond with her child. Other caregivers will do much of the imprinting, and the mother can only hope that she has chosen people who are stable, loving, and capable.[7]

Who's Minding the Children?

For years, the debate has continued about the pros and cons of the working mother. According to the National Center for Education Statistics, in 1995 there were approximately 21 million infants, toddlers, and preschool children under

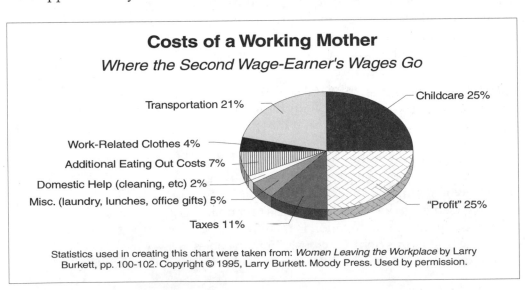

Costs of a Working Mother
Where the Second Wage-Earner's Wages Go

Childcare 25%

Transportation 21%

Work-Related Clothes 4%

Additional Eating Out Costs 7%

Domestic Help (cleaning, etc) 2%

Misc. (laundry, lunches, office gifts) 5%

Taxes 11%

"Profit" 25%

Statistics used in creating this chart were taken from: *Women Leaving the Workplace* by Larry Burkett, pp. 100-102. Copyright © 1995, Larry Burkett. Moody Press. Used by permission.

the age of six in the United States; more than 12.9 million (61 percent) of these children were in childcare outside the home.[8]

However, something has been happening in the last few years. Research conducted by Richard Hokenson and based on Bureau of Labor statistics suggests that women of childbearing age have been leaving their jobs and returning home in significant numbers. The reason, says Hokenson, is that "on average, 80 percent of a working mother's paycheck goes to support her children, with childcare the major cost."[9]

A survey of 801 homes across America by Larry Burkett's organization, Christian Financial Concepts, came up with very similar statistics.

When these facts are combined with the emotional cost of being separated from their children during their most impressionable years, it is no wonder that the number of people working at home in some fashion has risen from 2.5 million in 1975 to 52 million in 1997.[10] Many of these are mothers who found a way to return home to be the primary caretaker of their children.

Work together with your spouse or someone in similar circumstances and see how your costs compare to Larry Burkett's research. If you are a one-income family, list your monthly budget in all applicable areas, and circle those areas in which you feel the most stressed by having only one wage earner.

	Amount	Percent

Expenses Paid by First/Only Income

    Charitable contributions

    Housing

    Food

    Transportation

    Taxes

    Clothing

    Lessons

    Vacation/Leisure

    Other

Additional Expenses for Working Single Parent or Second Income

    Childcare

    Transportation

    Work clothing

    Meals out/ordered

    Domestic help

    Miscellaneous (see chart)

    Taxes

    Profit to help with . . .

Good Mothering Is Every Child's Birthright

It may be true that some men are staying home and doing a credible job of nurturing their children, but I believe they are adapting to a role that is far better suited to the mother, particularly when children are very young. Dr. Brenda Hunter, a psychologist who specializes in infant attachment and the effects of infant daycare on children, makes the basic difference between men and women one of the key premises in her book, *Home by Choice*.

Hunter recalls what it was like to be raised by her own mother, who worked full time.[11] Not surprisingly, she became a working mother during the growing-up years of her own two daughters. Then in her forties, having earned a degree in psychology that introduced her to the fascinating and highly complex nature of infants and the attachments they form with their parents, she realized the mistakes she had made as a mother, as well as her own mother's mistakes, by being out of the home too much. Hunter became convinced that "good mothering is every child's birthright."[12]

Note-it

Imprinting, especially by the mother as she bonds with her baby, is critical during the first months and years of life. A baby's emotional bond or attachment to its mother is what one psychiatrist calls "the foundation stone of personality."

In her book, Hunter frequently mentions the work of British psychiatrist John Bowlby, who wrote about the centrality of a baby's emotional bond or attachment to his mother. Bowlby calls this bond the "foundation stone of personality," and he goes on to say, "The young child's hunger for his mother's love and presence is as great as his hunger for food. When mother isn't there, the child inevitably generates a powerful sense of loss and anger."[13]

The Working Mom

I realize I've made a strong case for moms to stay home in order to imprint their children at every opportunity. But some of you don't have a choice, so I don't want you to get the idea that a working mom can't imprint her children at all. She can do a great deal—it will just take more planning, effort, and sacrifice. The childcare agency or caregiver will do some imprinting, but a working mom can do several things to make the situation as positive as possible. If you are in this situation, consider the following options, which I call "the positive side of working."

Consider Working at Home

The advantages are obvious: You're close to your children, you avoid the commuter hassle, your hours can be flexible, and, if you are in business for yourself, your overhead should be low. Some home-based businesses still require you to use occasional childcare while you meet with clients or go to appointments, but the amount of time away from your children can be greatly reduced. Perhaps best of all, your newfound flexibility allows you to avoid those inevitable moments when you get the "guilties" after dropping off your ill or unhappy child at a daycare center.[14]

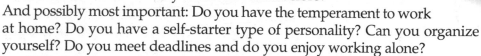

Note-it

If possible, only one parent should work during a child's growing-up years, which extend at least through junior high. If both parents must work or if you are a single parent, make every effort to get the best child-care you can possibly find.

Before launching a work-at-home career, study a book like Larry Burkett's *Women Leaving the Work Place* or Brenda Hunter's *Home by Choice*, which will walk you through some of the critical questions you need to ask: What do you really enjoy doing? Do other people see you with any particular skills and talents? Do you have any talents that are hidden or that you haven't tried before? And possibly most important: Do you have the temperament to work at home? Do you have a self-starter type of personality? Can you organize yourself? Do you meet deadlines and do you enjoy working alone?

With the advent of personal computers, many people are able to work at home for other companies either on a part-time or full-time basis. Also, more people are choosing to job-sequence their career and family. That is, they put their career on hold while they raise their children and then go back to work outside the home. Supreme Court Justice Sandra Day O'Connor is a good example of this.

Working at home isn't for everyone. Some women have tried it and decided it was better to go back to the office. But if it works for you, you can turn it into something beneficial for you and your child.

If Working at Home Isn't Possible

If working at home just isn't feasible, *consider taking your child to work*. I know of moms who bundle their babies up in the morning and take them down to the office or the store, complete with portable crib or playpen. There they tend to their jobs and their children throughout the day. I've seen this done in a flower shop and in a fabric store. Again, this isn't for everyone. You would need the kind of job where you could be interrupted—sometimes frequently—by your child and be able to tend to his or her needs. But the point is: some people are doing it. Perhaps you could, too.

Sounds nice, you say, but children aren't allowed at your place of business. What do you do then?

- *Consider part-time work* (and thus part-time childcare). Part-time work usually means no benefits like retirement or medical insurance, but if these things can be covered by your spouse's income or in some other way, part-time work does mean more time at home with your children.

- *Consider in-home childcare if you can afford it.* A grandparent or other trusted extended family member can never replace mom or dad but may be the next best thing. Or an at-home mom may be "working at home" by providing childcare. Finding someone you trust with similar values is important.
- *If you use a daycare center, do your homework!* See the following "Checklist for Finding Good Childcare," for things to consider when choosing daycare for your child.

Checklist for Finding Good Childcare[20]

1. The facility should have flexible visitation rules that allow parents to come in and observe at any time. In addition, it should have a good security plan that includes a sign-in/sign-out system so that no one can walk in off the street posing as a friend or relative to pick up a child.

2. Reputable facilities check out their employees. This can include an FBI check of fingerprints or at least a check with the local police department. The obvious reason for this kind of check is to be sure the facility isn't hiring a known pedophile or person with some other criminal record.

3. The facility should have a clear-cut policy for dismissing the children. Who picks up the children each day? In these days of rampant divorce and separation, all childcare/ preschool facilities need to be extremely careful. Some facilities even require lists of people who are not allowed to pick up the child under any circumstances.

4. The physical condition and appearance of the facilities are extremely important. Are they neat and clean? Is equipment clean and up-to-date? Are there colorful decorations? Are there plenty of toys that are clean and in good repair: blocks, dolls, trucks, cars, balls, and the like? Also, what about hands-on stuff such as clay, sand, watercolors—anything that allows children to be creative? Ask yourself, "If I were four years old, would I want to play here?"

5. What are the facility's emergency procedures in case of an accident or sudden illness? And what are the policies concerning children who are ill or who are coming down with something? Stay away from facilities that are too permissive about taking half-sick children. Some schools or agencies may have areas where they can isolate children who aren't feeling well, but the best place for a sick child is home in bed.

6. What are the credentials of staff members? This is especially important regarding preschools,

---

No matter how much you have to work or what options you choose, *always let your children know how much you love them—every day.* Help them understand why you have to go to work. Make sure they know that being away from them is not what you really want to do. Your children are your first choice, but you don't have that choice right now. Also, a working mom needs to budget her time carefully. Let some of the housework go, if necessary, to focus on your children. No matter how challenging a situation might be, the important thing is that your children feel loved.

but it doesn't hurt to ask for credentials, or at least experience records, on daycare workers. The point is, do the people who are going to be taking care of your child know what they are doing? Also, keep in mind that turnover is usually much greater in child-care facilities than it is in preschools. Occasionally you will find some preschool workers who have been with a facility for many years.

7. What are the facility's policies regarding discipline of children? Does the director of the facility allow any staff member to yell, scream, or use heavy-handed punitive measures with the children? This is extremely difficult to ascertain in one interview or one phone call. If at all possible, try to spend some time at the facility, observing what goes on before enrolling your child there on a permanent basis. Ideally, you should try to spend the entire day and see what happens with children of all ages. Of course, staff workers will be on their best behavior while you are there, but you can still learn quite a bit about how patient they are and how they react to various situations. Note especially whether the smaller children, including infants, are held and talked to. Beware of any facility that is hesitant to allow you to come and observe. If you feel you are not welcome, try somewhere else.

8. What is the ratio of adult staff members to children? As a rule, with two- and three-year-old children, there should be no more than eight children in the care of each adult staff member.

(NOTE: If your child is a little older and you are considering preschool, check out the guidelines I provide beginning on page 100 in my book *Bringing Up Kids Without Tearing Them Down.*)

What About Dad?

I've spent a lot of time focusing on how important mothers are in a child's life. Does this mean that Dad is off the parenting hook, free to concentrate on his career and cure his slice? Not on your pacifier! Dad plays an equally important but different role in the task of parenting, which ideally is a team operation. Everything I say in this book is based on that idea of teamwork. The best upbringing a child can have is by *both parents* who are dedicated to each other and to their task.

Dads, love your wives! As badly as children need the love of their parents, they have an even greater need to see their parents loving each other. Research shows that when asked what they fear the most, children don't list nuclear war or stranger-danger. Their major fear is that "Mommy and Daddy might get a divorce."

It doesn't matter if you have a two-career family, a one-and-a-half-career family, or a one-career family. None of these works well unless Mom and Dad remember where their real priorities must lie—in loving each other and then loving their children with everything they've got.

Dads, make time for your children! Open the "month-at-a-glance" calendar (or its equivalent) of an effective father (and mother, too) and you will see certain dates blocked out. Depending on the time of year, it will say "Johnny's Little League game, 2:00 P.M.," "Janie's soccer game, 9:00 A.M.," "Trent's band concert, 10:00 A.M." Whatever little Johnny or Janie or Trent is doing, Mom and Dad will have it written down, and they'll plan to be there. Also penciled into the date book will be the children's award ceremonies, birthdays, and graduations, not to mention some one-on-one "dates" for breakfast out or a Saturday bike ride or overnight campout. Remember, children will always value your "presence" more than your "presents."

Kids are dying to belong. They want to belong to something. Most kids start off wanting to belong to their family. But families—quite frankly—are so hecticly institutionalized that they have forked their kids over to strangers at an early age. If kids can't belong to the family, they can certainly find a gang that will welcome them.

Dads, being there for your children doesn't get less important as the children grow older. In fact, it can become even more demanding. You can't tell yourself that you're going to concentrate on your children the first few months or years of their lives and *then* you can ease off. Your availability must continue throughout their lives if you want to imprint them in a way that builds self-image and a sense of self-worth. In fact, the older children get, the more dates get filled in on your calendar. Children need love all their lives. As they grow older, it takes more, not less, love to fill their emotional tanks.

Dads (and Moms), quality comes out of quantity! One of the scourges of our age is the term "quality time." I'm not sure who coined those words, but it's my guess they didn't spend much time with their children, so they dreamed up a mythical concept that "quality" is better than "quantity." Quality time is based on the presupposition that you don't have much time to spend with your children. Therefore you "put everything you've got" into the few minutes you have. This may be true for some people, but for a lot of people, quality time is not only a myth, it's a cop-out.

The truth is, quality moments with your child don't happen on cue. They happen of their own accord while you're spending time together. I'm a firm believer in spending as much time as I can with my kids in the hope that the quality moments will happen. We all have the same amount of time in the day. The question is: how will we use it?

In the godly family, the priorities are clear: People—particularly family people—are more important than meetings, sales reports, golf games, work-late days, luncheons, or shopping expeditions. Functional parents value their family, and they live out that value every day.[15]

Time Robbers

Work isn't the only culprit that robs us of time with our children. Parents and children can be in the same house at the same time and still not be spending any time together. Television is a common "time robber." So are too many evening meetings, dinners on the run, frequent work-related travel, kids' activities spent elsewhere, and separate activities on weekends.

 Take a few minutes to evaluate where the time goes in your house. Then jot down the ideal amount of time for that activity.

	Time Spent	
	Actual	Ideal
Hours TV is on daily (average)		
Evening meetings per week		
Meals together per week		
Nights away from home per month (for example, work travel)		
Church activities per week		
Kids, nights out per week		
Parents, nights out per week		
Evenings whole family is home		
Other: _____		

Tim Hansel, author of *What Kids Need Most in a Dad*,[16] found an article that said, "If you're thirty-five, you have only five hundred days left to live." The writer of the article pointed out that if a person subtracts the time spent working, engaging in personal hygiene, cleaning house, and doing all the odd jobs of life, that person has five hundred days left to live as he or she chooses.

Stunned by this revelation, Hansel decided to develop some statistics for the amount of parenting time he had. Figuring that a parent has children from birth to age eighteen and giving a parent one hour a day talking with his or her children, he came out with 273 days that parents have to spend with each child.[17] (One hour a day may have been generous given the fact that some studies suggest fathers spend no more than thirty-seven seconds a day in focused conversation with their children.[18])

 Psalm 90:12 says, "Teach us to number our days aright, that we may gain a heart of wisdom." In this case, the wisdom to be gained concerns how you spend time with your children. Calculate how many days you have left to spend with each of your children.

Child's Name	Years Remaining (18 - present age)	Hours Remaining (x 365)	Days Remaining (÷ 24 hours)
• *Sample three-year-old*	*15*	*5,475*	*228*
•			
•			
•			
•			
•			

I don't know about you, but when I realize that I have (in some cases had) only 273 days to parent each of my children, the distinctions between quality time and quantity time get pretty blurred. Therefore, I want to spend all the time I can with each child, and that's why that date book becomes so important.

A Message for All Moms and Dads

I don't know the ages of your children. They may all be quite young, and you have a lot of imprinting to do. Perhaps they are teenagers heading out of the nest and your imprinting opportunities are just about over. One thing I do know: *The geese are on the lawn.* If imprinting doesn't happen now, it won't happen later. There is no remedial goose school, and the saddest words a parent could ever utter are "If only I had spent more time with my children when I had the chance."

Whatever the age of your children, there is still time to imprint their minds and hearts with your love and guidance. You are the one to show them the way home.[19]

If you've been remiss about spending time with your children and you know you haven't done what you should have, you might start with an apology and tell them that from now on things are going to be different.

 Pair with another couple (or three to four single parents) in similar circumstances (working parents, at-home mom, work at home, and so on). Regardless of your circumstances, consider and discuss the following questions.

1. What are the daily times spent together with my children that I feel most positive about? Weekly? (Dad? Mom?)

2. What one-on-one times do I spend with each of my children on a daily basis? Weekly? (Dad? Mom?)

3. What kinds of time spent with my children do I feel are lacking? (With children together? One on one? Time with Dad? Time with Mom?)

4. What would have to change in my work, lifestyle, or weekly schedule to carve out more time with my children?

5. What are the obstacles to making such a change?

6. In what *one positive way* can I commit myself to spending more time with my children in the coming week? (Do this individually at the end of your group discussion.) Write that commitment here:

 Pray for one another in your small sharing groups that God will show you ways to create more time with your children and give you the courage to make the needed changes.

Portions of this session were adapted from:
Leman, Dr. Kevin. *Bringing Up Kids Without Tearing Them Down* (chapter 4). Nashville, Tenn.: Nelson, 1995.

For further information, consider:

Burkett, Larry. *Women Leaving the Workplace.* Chicago: Moody, 1995.

Hansel, Tim. *What Kids Need Most in a Dad.* Old Tappan, N.Y.: Revell, 1984.

Hunter, Brenda. *Home by Choice.* Portland, Ore.: Multnomah, 1991.

Kesler, Jay, with Ronald Beers and LaVonne Neff, eds. *Parents and Children.* Wheaton, Ill.: Victor, 1986.

Leman, Dr. Kevin. *Bringing Up Kids Without Tearing Them Down.* Video series. © 1994 by Dallas Christian Video.

Ziglar, Zig. *Raising Positive Kids in a Negative World.* Nashville, Tenn.: Nelson, 1985.

NOTES

1. "Flying with Geese: Blending Science, Art," Geographica, *National Geographic,* May 1991.
2. Adapted from Dr. Kevin Leman, *Bringing Up Kids Without Tearing Them Down* (Nashville, Tenn.: Nelson, 1995), p. 77.
3. Richard I. Evans, *Konrad Lorenz: The Man and His Ideas* (New York: Harcourt Brace Jovanovich, 1975), p. 13.
4. Quoted in Evans.
5. Evans, pp. 14-16.
6. These studies include the work of Marshall Klaus and John Kennell of Case Western Reserve School of Medicine, Cleveland, Ohio. See Zig Ziglar, *Raising Positive Kids in a Negative World* (Nashville, Tenn.: Nelson, 1985), p. 110.
7. Adapted from Dr. Kevin Leman, *Bringing Up Kids . . .,* p. 78.
8. "Child Care for Young Children: Demographics," *Child Care Bulletin,* September/October 1997, Issue 17. Published by the National Child Care Information Center, U.S. Department of Health and Human Services.
9. Leith Anderson, "Clocking Out," *Christianity Today,* 12 September 1994, pp. 30-32.
10. Harriet Webster, "Would You Like to Work at Home?" *Reader's Digest,* March 1998, p. 130, citing a 1997 study by Find/SVP, a New York research firm.
11. Brenda Hunter, *Home by Choice* (Portland, Ore.: Multnomah, 1991), pp. 32-33.
12. Hunter, p. 35.
13. John Bowlby, *Attachment,* vol. 1 of *Attachment and Loss,* 2d ed. (New York: Basic Books, 1982), p. 177. Quoted by Hunter, *Home by Choice,* p. 26, referenced in Dr. Kevin Leman, *Bringing Up Kids Without Tearing Them Down,* p. 82.
14. Adapted from Dr. Kevin Leman, *Bringing Up Kids . . . ,* pp. 87-88.
15. Leman, Dr. Kevin *Bringing Up Kids. . .,* pp. 90-93.
16. Tim Hansel, *What Kids Need Most in a Dad* (Old Tappan, N.Y.: Revell, 1984).
17. See Tim Hansel, "Quality Time Versus Quantity Time," in *Parents and Children,* Jay Kesler, Ron Beers, and LaVonne Neff, eds. (Wheaton, Ill.: Victor, 1986), p. 90.
18. Josh McDowell, "Creative Parenting—How to Be a Hero to Your Kids" (Lubbock, Tex.: Liberation Tapes, 9 October 1985). McDowell cites two studies: one in a Midwestern town among three hundred seventh and eighth graders and another in a southern Michigan town among a hundred preschoolers wired with mikes.
19. Adapted from Dr. Kevin Leman, *Bringing Up Kids . . . ,* pp. 94, 96-97.
20. Leman, pp. 99-100.

PART TWO

Bringing Up Kids Without Tearing Them Down

"Who Do You Think You Are, Anyway?"
The Importance of Self-Esteem

Want to have a dog?
  "Gotta get a dog license."
Want to drive a car?
  "Gotta get a driver's license."
Want to go duck hunting?
  "Gotta get a hunting license."
Want to practice law in this state?
  "Gotta get a state license."
Want to become a parent?
  "Uh . . . just do it."

It's ironic that in our society we need a license for just about anything—even keeping a dog—but there are no "parent licenses" being issued that I know of. Parents are expected to "wing it," and they muddle along, hoping that if they just "love little Buford enough," everything will come out okay.

Well, everything isn't coming out okay. Millions of kids are growing up with a poor self-image, lacking good feelings about themselves.[1] We have teenage girls, who don't feel loved and accepted, having babies just so they'll have someone to love and love them in return. We have boys and young men joining gangs in record numbers because a gang is like a "family," and they gain a sense of identity and belonging. We have kids who have been labeled failures, so they turn to violence and crime as a way to make them feel like "somebody" and get "respect."

Of course, not all kids go to these extremes. But even the average teenager who struggles with her self-image learns the trick of building herself up by putting others down. And every generation has its share of frenetic go-getters who are always trying to prove their worth by what they *do*, rather than feeling secure in who they *are*.

Self-image Is Important

The way we act even from our earliest years is tied to our self-image. Our self-image is how we see or picture ourselves. If we see ourselves as losers, we'll be losers. If we think we count only when we're in control, we'll turn out to be pushy, overly aggressive, dominating, and insensitive. If we believe we are loved and accepted, we'll be much more apt to love and accept other people as well.

As Dr. Don Dinkmeyer, a colleague from whom I have learned much about parenting children, says: "A child who sees himself as worthwhile and useful [is less likely] to develop destructive patterns. He does not turn to drugs and rebellion. He possesses a cooperative spirit, a sense of responsibility, and positive attitudes toward his family. His relationship with his parents is one of mutual trust and respect."[2]

Sounds good! And yet a lot of parents still feel uneasy, as if emphasizing positive self-esteem flies in the face of our Christian values of humility, servanthood, and putting others first. Or we're afraid that building up our children's self-esteem will make them prideful or egotistical or self-centered. And we rightfully squirm when our society takes a good concept and runs wild with it, lowering academic standards so "everyone passes," considering everyone's viewpoint as "equally valid" (whether it's satanic rituals or violent rock lyrics), and thinking every lifestyle and perspective must be treated "without bias" (no convictions about "right" and "wrong" allowed). After all, we don't want anyone to feel bad, right?

Some time ago, during a speech at commencement exercises for Brown University, a professor made this surprisingly candid statement.

> We, the faculty, take no pride in our educational achievements with you. . . . With us you could argue about why your errors were not our errors, why mediocre work really was excellent, why you could take pride in routine and slipshod presentation. For four years we created an altogether forgiving world, in which whatever slight effort you gave was all that was demanded. When you did not keep appointments, we made new ones. When your work came in beyond deadline, we pretended not to care.
>
> Why? Despite your fantasies, it was not even that we wanted to be liked by you. It was that we did not want to be bothered, and the easy way out was pretense: smiles and easy Bs.
>
> Few professors actually care whether or not they are liked by peer-paralyzed adolescents, fools so shallow as to imagine professors care not about education but about popularity. It was, again, to be rid of you. So go, unlearn the lies we taught you.[3]

Like all aspects of parenting, building your child's self-esteem must find a healthy balance of helping him or her feel secure, loved, accepted, and worthwhile without raising a selfish kid who thinks he or she is the center of the universe and should be allowed to say or do anything he or she wants regardless of the consequences.

 As a supplement to this session, view "The Seeds of Self-Esteem" on the videotape, *Bringing Up Kids Without Tearing Them Down,* © 1994 by Dallas Christian Video.

Self-Image and Jesus' Relationship with His Father

What can we learn about positive self-image from the life of Jesus—who, though He was fully God, came to earth fully human and experienced life and its challenges "in every way, just as we [do]" (Hebrews 4:15)—and His relationship with God the Father?

 Gather in small groups of four and explore the following Scriptures, deciding together which statement on the right is best illustrated by the biblical texts. (Answer key can be found on page 121)

Match the following:
(NOTE: some texts will illustrate more than one statement.)

(a) Matthew 16:13-20;
   John 10:24-30; 13:13

(b) Matthew 3:17; 17:5

(c) Matthew 26:6-10

(d) Mark 2:15-17

(e) Matthew 28:18

(f) John 15:9

(g) Luke 2:48-50

(h) John 10:30; 17:21

___ 1. He knew He was loved by His Father.
___ 2. He could love others because He was secure in the love of His Father.
___ 3. His relationship with His Father gave Him purpose in life.
___ 4. He was affirmed by His Father.
___ 5. He was secure in His identity.
___ 6. His positive sense of self allowed Him to withstand criticism.
___ 7. His positive sense of self allowed Him to relate to those less fortunate, rather than building His image by relating only to the rich and powerful.
___ 8. He knew He belonged to His Father.
___ 9. He felt competent and equipped by His Father to do what He needed to do.

Come back together as a large group and briefly discuss the following questions growing out of the Bible study.

1. What is the significance of God the Father acknowledging His "beloved Son" *before* Jesus had begun His earthly ministry?

2. What else can we learn about relating to our own children by understanding how God the Father related to His Son Jesus?

3. What can we learn about our own identity and sense of worth as children of God?

4. Do these verses raise any questions for you about identity and self-esteem?

Self-Image Is as Basic as ABC

As parents, many of us take out health insurance as protection for the future of our family. I'd like to introduce another kind of future investment: Image Insurance. The up-front premiums are pretty basic, but the dividends and payback are fantastic. I call them the ABCs of self-worth.[4] Although they may sound simple, building them into your child takes time—a lifetime, to be exact.

"A" Is for Acceptance and Affirmation

Children who feel accepted and affirmed tell themselves, "Hey, Mom and Dad love me, no matter what. They really care about *me*." Acceptance means being loved unconditionally for who you are, not for how you perform or what you do. Affirmation helps a child know he or she is valued as a unique individual, not in comparison to someone else.

I cohost a daily program that's heard throughout the country. During a broadcast on the subject of self-image and building a good sense of self-worth, a woman called in to say this:

> This is one area that I'm glad my mom and dad did a great job in. . . . I am not a very quiet person. I was not petite. I was not blond. I was not a cheerleader. You know, I wasn't any of those neat things, but, boy, I had music, and I could do plays at school, and they encouraged me every day

to do my best in those things. And they came, and they were there. And I think that has been the secret with my own children. Not only did my husband and I tell them to go out and do it, but also I think you need to be there for them.

This mother was describing what acceptance and affirmation is all about. To *be there*, to encourage, to hug, to support. All this should start early in a child's life—the earlier the better.

"B" Is for Belonging

Belonging is the other side of the acceptance coin. While acceptance affirms that you are a person of value for who you are as an individual, belonging affirms your identity as an important part of the group. A feeling of belonging is one of the earliest building blocks in anyone's self-image. It gives a child roots and a sense of security in the family unit. When a child feels he belongs, he tells himself, "I am worth something to someone. I'm important. I fit in." When the sense of belonging is strong and secure, then a child can risk exploring his or her individuality. When the sense of belonging is weak, a child often will try desperately to "fit in" in ways that are inappropriate, maybe stifling parts of himself that cause rejection or feeling "responsible" for whether the family is holding together.

> ### Note-it
> The ABCs of self-worth are feeling that you are accepted, feeling that you belong, and feeling that you are capable.

Children don't get very far in life before they run smack into situations where they're on the outside looking in. They aren't welcome in the "in group." Maybe they find themselves without any friends or anyone to talk to. It's bound to happen sometime to just about every kid. If the sense of belonging in the family is strong, children can weather these disappointments. But if the sense of belonging is weak, a child—especially when he or she hits the teen years—is going to look elsewhere for that sense of belonging.

How many of you have watched with horror as a new child comes into a group situation—whether it be at school or at play—and within the first few minutes the child turns the group against him? Well, why do children do such things? Why do some children just naturally stack the deck against themselves? Why? Because in their own minds, they're not worthy of being loved. When someone reaches out to accept them, they reject it. You sometimes see this scenario when a loving, caring family adopts a child who previously has been abused. Often such a child will go out of his or her way to show the adoptive parents that he or she is not worth loving.

"C" Is for Competence

Children with a good self-image feel capable. They face a challenge and tell themselves, "I can do it!" This is *not* the same as feeling that one's self-worth is based only on how well you perform or the things you can *do*. Rather, a sense of competence has more to do with one's identity as a capable, worthy person. Parents can help instill this identity as they encourage, support, and say, "Go for it! You can do it!"

Note-it

Children with healthy self-images are responsible and capable, confident but not cocky, sensitive to the needs of others but not doormats, always trying to do their best but not hung up on perfectionism.

As children grow, they will inevitably come face to face with their own weaknesses and limitations. If they are ridiculed for these failings or if parents say, "Oh, you can't do anything right!" they will quickly learn to see themselves as failures. But if they are helped to see that weaknesses can be overcome and are assured that they also possess real strengths and abilities, they'll become persons who aren't afraid to try.

There is nothing like the sense of satisfaction and fulfillment that comes with being able to say, "I did it!"—however simple or small the accomplishment. Actually doing something makes you feel worthwhile and capable. One of my early memories is of playing softball at the age of five with my uncles and other members of our family. I clearly recall hitting the ball and running around the bases *twice.* In retrospect, it's obvious that my uncles and the other older players deliberately missed the ball or made wild throws, and then they smiled as they watched a little five-year-old dash determinedly around the bases. I didn't realize what they were up to, of course, but I can tell you that it felt like a million dollars.

Divide into three subgroups. Each group should take one of the ABCs of self-worth (Acceptance and Affirmation; Belonging; and Competence) and brainstorm possible ways you can instill that dimension of self-esteem in your children in everyday family life for different ages: preschool, elementary, junior high, high school. Don't take more than five minutes for this brainstorming activity. Remember that it's not what they do but who they are.

Come back together as a large group. Each group should share some of the ideas you generated. Use the space on the next page to jot down ideas from each brainstorming group for the different ages of children.

Acceptance/Affirmation	Belonging	Competence

Preschool

Elementary

Junior High

High School

A Good Self-Image Is Priceless

The ABCs of self-worth add up to a healthy self-image. As Dorothy Briggs points out in her book, *Your Child's Self-Esteem*, "Children have two basic needs. Their self-respect is based on two convictions: I am lovable and I am worthwhile."[5]

When a healthy self-image gives you high feelings of self-worth, it is what Nathaniel Branden in *The Psychology of Self-Esteem* calls "the integrated sum of self-confidence and self-respect. It is the conviction that one is competent to live and worthy of living."[6]

A good self-image is a priceless possession, but the concept still worries and even frightens some parents. When I speak at seminars and workshops and mention self-image and helping our kids feel like "somebody," some parents respond with reservations they've been taught by *their* parents: Won't all this talk about self-image and self-worth make a child self-indulgent, self-serving, and just plain selfish? Won't building up a child's self-image backfire and turn out an arrogant little brat who grows up to be a conceited adult?

To this kind of nonsense I say, "Bullcrumble!" Arrogant little brats grow into conceited adults because of having a *poor* self-image, not a *good* one. A healthy self-image doesn't *breed* selfishness or arrogance. It *prevents* it.[7]

A Poor Self-Image Can Lead to Real Trouble

Youngsters who grow up feeling they are "nothing" or "worthless"—whether that message comes to them from their parents or from mainstream society, which has "written off" certain segments of the youth population—become troubled kids who struggle in school and have difficulty making friends. Or they make the wrong kind of friends who have similar problems. Often they grow up living fearful, insecure, defeated lives. Some are so hungry for affirmation and attention, they act out in destructive ways. After all, negative attention is better than no attention at all! Numerous studies show that our prisons are full of youngsters, as well as men and women, who grew up feeling they were nothing and nobody. To become somebody they turned to crime or gangs, creating their own

Note-it

Giving children opportunities to give back to the family is fundamental to building a healthy self-image. When children see themselves as worthwhile and useful, they have no need to develop negative attitudes and destructive behavior.

negative social system of acceptance, affirmation, belonging, and competence.

Today, few would argue with the fact that *every* child in America is in danger of being tempted by, and possibly succumbing to, the use of drugs. One of the key reasons many children get hooked is because they feel they aren't accepted, that they don't belong, that they can't do much of anything. All this adds up to feeling worthless. They are offered drugs by people who promise them good times, friends, and plenty of kicks. It's no wonder kids try drugs. Why not? Here is their ticket to being *accepted,* to feeling that they *belong.*

You may be thinking that your child is in no danger, but please think again. A positive self-image isn't simply an option, something we want to work on like being sure the child learns phonics. *A positive self-image is a must.*

What About Your Own Self-Image?

It's not unusual for parents to say, "I'd like to help my child have a good self-image, but I don't have a great one myself. My own parents (or teachers, coaches, and others) made me feel worthless a lot of the time."

How can we build a good self-image in each one of our children if our own self-image makes us feel like dandelions on the lawn of life? I wish I could send parents out to buy an Image Insurance policy that would take care of everything, but that's not the way it works. Concepts such as "self-image" and "self-worth" are relatively easy to describe, but raising children to have strong feelings of self-worth is difficult and demanding. Parents who come to me for help often admit that they don't know how to "do it right." And why should they? They have had no training for what just might be the most challenging task in all of life—parenting.

It's true enough that many of us have grown up with a poor self-image and now, as adults, we're "getting by." Some of us may have learned to conquer feelings of low self-worth, and we're functioning fairly well. But how much better it would be to have grown up feeling affirmed and accepted, as if we belonged somewhere, and were encouraged to feel competent and capable, able to do whatever we set our minds to.

One thing I try to instill in parents I'm working with is the concept of cognitive self-discipline. That is, when they have negative thoughts, it's time to stop and ask themselves if they are telling themselves the truth about who they are. If they are Christian parents who love God, then they need to say, "This is a lie I'm telling myself. God loves me." In private practice over the years, many, many times I've asked adults to pray while looking into a mirror asking God to help them love themselves as they know God loves them.

A Biblical Foundation for Self-Esteem

Although we can't rewrite the past, the good news is that God's relationship with us gives us a whole new basis for how we see ourselves, giving us the resources not only to change the present for ourselves but to help us raise our kids for the future.

> Choose one or more of the following sets of verses to look up, working either individually or with several others. Make sure all sets are assigned. Identify essential biblical truth for your set of verses and what this truth means for your self-esteem.

Set 1: John 3:16; 1 John 4:10

- Biblical truth: ■ Implication for self-esteem:

Set 2: Romans 3:23-26; 5:6-9; 8:1-4

- Biblical truth: ■ Implication for self-esteem:

Set 3: Genesis 1:26-27; Psalm 8:4-5; Isaiah 43:7

- Biblical truth: ■ Implication for self-esteem:

Set 4: Psalm 8:6-8; Hebrews 2:7-8

- Biblical truth: ■ Implication for self-esteem:

Set 5: Ezekiel 34:11-5; John 10:14-15,27-29

■ Biblical truth: ■ Implication for self-esteem:

Set 6: Romans 12:4-5; 1 Corinthians 12:14-27

■ Biblical truth: ■ Implication for self-esteem:

Set 7: John 1:12; 1 Peter 2:9; 1 John 3:1; 1 John 5:19

■ Biblical truth: ■ Implication for self-esteem:

Set 8: Acts 1:8; 2 Corinthians 12:9; Ephesians 3:20; Philippians 4:13

■ Biblical truth: ■ Implication for self-esteem:

Set 9: Romans 8:38-39

■ Biblical truth: ■ Implication for self-esteem:

Set 10: Psalm 37:5-6

■ Biblical truth: ■ Implication for self-esteem:

 Gather back together in the large group. Volunteers can read your set of verses and your conclusions regarding the primary biblical truth and its implication for your self-esteem. Share conclusions from all ten sets.

Five Principles of Image Insurance

If we have truly become "new creatures in Christ" and believe the biblical truths in this exercise, we can begin to see ourselves as God sees us, regardless of our past experiences. And as we incorporate these truths in our own hearts, they will become a foundation for how we relate to our own children.

Still, let's admit it: It's easy to feel defeated as parents when our children misbehave or we have a bad day. That's why I've developed Five Principles of Image Insurance for parents.[8] To begin with, when your children make mistakes, misbehave, or act as if they plan to make historians forget Attila the Hun, remember Image Insurance Principle 1.

1. Don't Take Misbehavior Personally

At crunch times—especially the "piranha hour" just before dinner—it helps to remember two things: (1) *All kids* misbehave and disobey at least occasionally and (2) *all parents* struggle at times with feeling inadequate and even worthless. There are no perfect parents, and when your children act less than perfectly (which is practically all the time), I repeat, *don't take it personally.* Simply realize that they are growing up, and they're being kids while they're at it.

I know this doesn't make their disobedience, laziness, forgetfulness, or what have you any less annoying or irritating, but it does help give you some perspective. And if you're not sinking into the muck hole of I-Must-Be-the-Worst-Parent-in-the-World or My-Kids-Are-Absolute-Slime, you might have time to wonder: Why does Billy refuse to do his homework? Why does Janie have such a messy room? Why is it seemingly impossible to get Billy and Janie to bed on time every evening?

Instead of wringing your hands over problems your children cause, stay calm, and remember Image Insurance Principle 2.

2. All Behavior Has a Purpose

Alfred Adler, the father of individual psychology, said that all human behavior has a goal of some kind. He said, "No human being could think, feel, will, dream without all these activities being determined, continued, modified, and directed toward an ever-present objective."[9] In other words, children choose certain behaviors because they get certain results that they want.

As a parent, be aware that your sweet little ankle-biters are always thinking, measuring, evaluating, and deciding how to act—or act up—to get what they want. When little Buford tries to drive big sister Hilda crazy with his pestering, you can be sure there is method in his madness. When Hilda doesn't come after being called to dinner for the fifteenth time, you can be sure she has her reasons.

Whatever little Buford or Hilda does or doesn't do, they are working out how they see life and how they see themselves fitting into life around them—particularly

in their family. To put it another way, everything Buford and Hilda does is a reflection of their self-image—how they picture themselves in their own little world.

All children soon develop their own idea of how to succeed and stand out. In effect, they decide how they are going to "make their reputation in the world." Don Dinkmeyer believes that whatever children choose to be, they want to be the best: "the greatest athlete, the most helpful girl in the class, or the cruelest boy in the block. Because we live in a culture that emphasizes the values of being superior in contrast to being equal, the child develops a reputation that gives him status, and then he behaves in ways that establish and fortify this image."[10]

If your child is misbehaving, one of the first things to look for is what motivates him or her to act in that manner. (We will deal with this in more depth in session 9.) Crucial to understanding your child is to learn *how a child thinks.* I like to say that we must "get behind a child's eyes." The more you can learn about how your children see life and how they are trying to meet their needs, the more you can do to change their behavior by directing their search for status and significance toward goals that are more productive, beneficent, and acceptable.

Once you master the first two principles, you're ready for Image Insurance Principle 3, the foundation of building a healthy self-image in any child.

3. Love Them No Matter What

Love your kids unconditionally—even when they're misbehaving. Unconditional love does *not* mean simply accepting or overlooking any behavior because you love your child. Unconditional love can help us deal with the misbehavior while still helping our child know how much we love him or her. Unconditional love is real, tough, and resilient, and "can cover a multitude of sins." But simply "hoping" it will happen doesn't do it. It will happen only if you make it happen.

Nobody—and I mean nobody—has cornered the market on achieving or even explaining unconditional love. Loving a child unconditionally is a beautiful ideal and a vital target for every parent to shoot for every day. Will you hit that target every time? Of course not, but the better you understand your children and why they act the way they do, the more frequently you will at least hit the outer ring of the target. Occasionally you will even hit the bull's-eye! The more often you hit the target of unconditional love, the better self-image your children will develop because they feel loved and secure, even during the difficult times when you would like to wring their precious little necks!

Another key to taking out image insurance on your children is to value them as they are, not as you would like them to be all the time. Never forget Image Insurance Principle 4.

4. Parents Don't Own Their Children

Remember in session 1 how we talked about not thinking that we owned our children so that we wouldn't slip into an authoritarian super-parent syndrome?

Well, here is another reason, this time related to Image Insurance for our children: *Each child is his or her own unique person, and he or she should be valued as such.*

Note-it

Acceptance means being loved unconditionally for who you are, not for how you perform or what you do. Affirmation helps a child know he or she is valued as a unique individual, not in comparison to someone else.

One of the best ways to value our children is to discover their assets and strengths and spend time encouraging and emphasizing them. It's absolutely imperative that we bring our children up positively, always finding and affirming the little things they do in life. Then, when children walk into that turbulent world called adolescence, they can say, "Hey, I'm Somebody."

For some kids, being "somebody" may mean blowing the tuba in the band at the Friday night football game. For others, it may mean being the point-after-touchdown specialist at that same game. Many kids, of course, are "just average," but they can all develop an interest, skill, or ability, from stamp collecting to building models, from earning their own spending money to developing their own neighborhood business (not the corner dealership in a certain white powder!) before they are seventeen.

If you value your children, you will affirm them constantly. If an apple a day keeps the doctor away, at least one positive statement every day to your child will certainly help keep a bad self-image at bay. In other words, bring your children up by building them up. Don't tear them down with a critical, negative attitude.

Yes, you will have to correct them when they are disobedient or irresponsible. But there are so many positive things you can say, so many words you can use that build children up rather than tear them down.

And when the time for discipline comes, keep Image Insurance Principle 5 in mind.

5. The Tail Does Not Wag the Dog

In session 3 we looked at three styles of parenting, two of which always contaminate the family: authoritarianism and permissiveness.

To avoid contamination and to keep the family on an even keel, it must be understood that no one member of the family is greater than the family as a whole.

Although in authority, neither Dad nor Mom can put personal desires ahead of the good of the entire family. And when it comes to the children, the tail must never wag the dog. When a child runs the show, he or she quickly becomes spoiled, which affects the whole family.

When children are raised permissively, they become particularly adept at disrupting schedules and routines to suit themselves. Mom may make scrambled eggs for breakfast, as she does every Tuesday, but little Harlan decides he wants buckwheat cakes. And so, wanting to please her little darling, Mom makes a special meal just for him. Another favorite battleground for children is bedtime or naptime. This is a battle well worth fighting, not only because children need their sleep, but also because it keeps children from thinking their agenda is more important than the rest of the family's.

> **Note-it**
>
> A feeling of belonging gives a child roots and a sense of security in the family unit. When the sense of belonging is strong and secure, a child can risk exploring his or her individuality.

Schedules and order are key tools in making sure the tail does not wag the dog. Remember, the whole is always greater than any of the parts—even darling little Harlan.

All the Dr. Kevin Leman kids have followed schedules, some of them more willingly than others. Holly, our tightly wired firstborn, was the hardest to convince that "It's time for a nap now." She fought every inch of the way and, even when she finally did take a nap, would wake up grumpier than before she went to sleep. No matter, we kept Holly on a schedule and it paid off. Today, as a high school English teacher, she still admits waking up isn't her favorite sport, but the sign on her classroom wall says it all: "Class rules: (1) Be on time. (2) Homework is to be done thoroughly. (3) Hand in work on time. (4) Be considerate of others. (5) Come prepared, ready to work."

Players on any team know that the whole is more important than the parts. This idea doesn't minimize any of the parts. In fact, the whole exists to allow every part to develop to its fullest potential toward personal fulfillment. In other words, when each part contributes to the success of the whole, each part enjoys greater feelings of healthy self-image and self-worth. To put it in terms of the ABCs of self-image, when each family member becomes responsible to and supportive of the whole family, then each family member enjoys feelings of acceptance, belonging, and competence.

To Respond Is Better Than to React

These five principles form a foundation for how to go about bringing up your kids without tearing them down. As you use these five principles, you will develop what Don Dinkmeyer calls a "response repertoire" for dealing with your children lovingly, consistently, and effectively. The better you understand your children's behavior, the more effectively you can parent them in the endless variety of situations that occur throughout the day.

When parenting, it's always better to respond to your child than to react.[11]

A response means that you are in control, that you are making choices, and that you aren't simply controlled by the same old knee-jerk reaction when children misbehave or just drive you a little crazy while they are acting like the children they are.

You can build your child's self-image without completely losing yours, but Image Insurance does have a price. It demands the very best you have to offer in commitment, dedication, and persistence. Many times you will think you are at war with your children. There is some truth to that. I often facetiously tell seminar crowds, "Children are the enemy." But, ironically, the real enemies are not our children. Pogo said it long ago: "We have met the enemy and he is us." We have to understand ourselves—where we came from, how our parents parented us, and who we have turned out to be. Then we'll be better prepared to understand our children and how we want to parent them.

 Together with your spouse—or with another single parent—use the following questions to help you evaluate and build self-esteem in your home.

Action Ideas

- How would I rate my own self-esteem growing up: Insecure? Moderately okay? Confident? Why?

- How would I rate my own self-esteem as a parent: Insecure? Moderately okay? Confident? Why?

- What Scriptures in this session are particularly helpful in building my sense of being a valuable person in God's sight?

- Is one of my children struggling with poor self-esteem? Why do I think this is so? What Scriptures could I share with this child to help him or her see himself or herself through God's eyes?

- How well am I practicing unconditional love with my children? Am I intimidated by this term, or am I willing to try to "love my kids no matter what"? When I fail to do so, am I willing to admit my errors, put them behind me, and try again?

- What can I do to help each of my children feel more accepted and affirmed?

- How do I build a sense of belonging in our family?

- How can I help my child feel capable and competent? Am I helping each of my children learn to be good at something, no matter how simple or ordinary it might be?

- In what specific ways do I try to treat each child as a unique person?

- In what specific way can I build each of my children's self-esteem in the coming week?

    Firstborn:

    Secondborn:

    Thirdborn:

    Fourthborn:

Answer key for "Self-Image and Jesus' Relationship with His Father" from page 107:

1(b); 2(f); 3(g); 4(b); 5(a); 6(c); 7(d); 8(h); 9(e)

Portions of this session were adapted from:

Leman, Dr. Kevin. *Bringing Up Kids Without Tearing Them Down* (chapter 1). Nashville, Tenn.: Nelson, 1995.

For further information, consider:

Branden, Nathaniel. *The Psychology of Self-Esteem.* New York: Bantam Books, 1971.

Briggs, Dorothy Corkille. *Your Child's Self-Esteem.* New York: Doubleday, 1975.

Campbell, Ross. *How to Really Love Your Child.* Wheaton, Ill.: Victor, 1977.

Ross. *How to Really Love Your Teenager.* Wheaton, Ill.: Victor, 1981.

Dinkmeyer, Don, and McKay, Gary. *Raising a Responsible Child: Practical Steps in Successful Family Relationships.* New York: Simon & Schuster, 1973.

Dobson, James C. *Hide or Seek.* Old Tappan, New Jersey: Revell Co., 1974.

Lewis, Robert. *Raising a Modern-Day Knight.* Colorado Springs, Colo.: Focus on the Family Pub., Dallas, Tex.: Distributed in the U.S. and Canada by Word, 1997.

NOTES

1. Adapted from Dr. Kevin Leman, *Bringing Up Kids Without Tearing Them Down* (Nashville, Tenn.: Nelson, 1995), p. 12.
2. Don Dinkmeyer and Gary McKay, *Raising a Responsible Child: Practical Steps in Successful Family Relationships* (New York: Simon & Schuster, 1973).
3. J. Neusner, quoted in Malcolm Stevenson Forbes, Jr., "As Undergraduates Recommence Their Efforts," *Forbes Magazine,* 26 October 1981.
4. Adapted from Dr. Kevin Leman, *Bringing Up Kids . . . ,* pp. 5-8.
5. Dorothy Corkille Briggs, *Your Child's Self-Esteem* (New York: Doubleday, 1975), pp.3-4.
6. Nathaniel Branden, *The Psychology of Self-Esteem* (New York: Bantam Books, 1971), p. 110.
7. Dr. Kevin Leman, *Bringing Up Kids . . .,* pp. 8-12.
8. Adapted from Dr. Kevin Leman, *Bringing Up Kids . . . ,* p. 12-19.
9. Alfred Adler, *Understanding Human Nature* (London: George Allen & Unwin, Ltd., 1928), p. 19.
10. Dinkmeyer and McKay, p. 27.
11. Adapted from Dr. Kevin Leman, *Bringing Up Kids . . . ,* p. 21.

Birth Order and Parenting:

Should You Treat All Your Children the Same?

As a seventeen-year-old high school student, I once was called on to give testimony in court concerning an auto accident I had witnessed. I remember thinking how odd it was that two other witnesses to the accident could be so blind. I *knew* I was right. The car at fault was the blue one, not the red one they had identified. And the blue car was headed east, not west!

Way back in high school, in that courtroom, I learned firsthand about the concept often called "the eye of the beholder." Parenting your child in a fair and effective way has its "eye of the beholder" element also. To be successful, you have to understand what reality is—particularly for your child. No matter what you, the adult, think or know about a given situation, as far as effective parenting is concerned, reality is how your child views that situation. What precisely happened, or what precisely is going on, is not really the issue. It is what a child *thinks* that counts. Your child's perception of what is happening is the reality you must deal with.[1]

We all know how important it is to avoid favoritism, but sometimes what seems like fairness to us—in fact, what may be identical treatment—isn't necessarily perceived that way by our children.

How have you dealt with this question of fairness and identical treatment in your family?

 On the scales on the next page, indicate the degree to which you agree or disagree with each statement.

Treating Them the Same/Different   **Seldom**   **Usually**

1. To be fair, I put all of the children
   to bed at the same time.

   1 ▬▬▬▬▬ 5

2. I rotate the chores equally
   among all of the children.

   1 ▬▬▬▬▬ 5

3. I sometimes take individual children on
   outings alone to give them special attention.

   1 ▬▬▬▬▬ 5

4. Whenever I give anyone a treat, I give
   them all the same treat.

   1 ▬▬▬▬▬ 5

5. To avoid pointing out the differences between
   my children, I try to keep the privileges or
   responsibilities the same for everyone
   regardless of age.

   1 ▬▬▬▬▬ 5

6. I'm careful not to give my younger
   children things (bicycles, privileges,
   and so on) at an earlier age than I gave
   them to my first child.

   1 ▬▬▬▬▬ 5

This questionnaire doesn't necessarily have any right or wrong answers that would apply to all families. It does, however, encourage you to think about how you have been approaching your children. And now, I would ask if you've been taking into consideration their birth order and how it affects their perception of the world?

Never Treat Them All the Same

Because of the impact of birth order, I sometimes say, "Never treat your children all the same." If you are like most parents, the idea of treating your children differently sounds like a recipe for disaster. But I'm not advocating any type of favoritism or unfairness. I'm simply suggesting that because of birth order and the difference in ages of your children, you will have an easier time as a parent if you don't treat them all the same, especially not at the same time.

Actually, many parents who think they are treating their children the same end up treating their children differently in ways I would never recommend. Take the example of the universal bedtime rule. For instance, in a family with three children—Roger, seven; Lisa, five; and Timmy, four—it may seem like equal treatment for them all to be hustled off to bed at 8:30. But chances are, when Roger was five, he had an 8 P.M. bedtime, and possibly an earlier one when he was younger. So are the children really being treated equally?

It is critical to understand that a child's order of birth has tremendous implications for how he or she learns and perceives reality. It is safe to say that each child perceives his or her family differently, because each child operates from a different vantage point within the family.

The key question for parents is not whether you are treating all your children the same, but "Are we aware of how each child experiences his or her place in the family so we can make each child feel loved and appreciated?"

In session 2 we learned about some of the characteristics children tend to exhibit according to their birth order. Now it is time to apply some of those insights to how we relate to each child as a unique person with particular needs.

This would be a good time to review "How to Make Your Child Feel Special" on the videotape, *Bringing Up Kids Without Tearing Them Down*, © 1994 by Dallas Christian Video. (You may have watched this in session 2, but it would be a good review of these concepts.)

Helping the Firstborn Chill Out

The biggest crisis any firstborn child faces is the reality of "dethronement," which occurs with the arrival of that new little brother or sister.

Firstborns are the center of attention for a relatively long time, as time is measured in a young child's life. In session 5 we explored how the first five to seven years of a child's life are the most important in developing the child's personality, character, and emotional makeup. If Mommy and Daddy don't have a second child until the firstborn is three years old, consider that three-fifths—60 percent—of the firstborn's most formative years occur before the intruder comes home from the hospital. Experience has taught the firstborn that he or she is kingpin. One of the most challenging tasks of parenting is preparing the firstborn child for the intrusion of the second.

Note-it

Have the oldest child put away some of his special toys in a safe place so the baby can't get them. This may sound silly to an adult, but to a three-year-old it makes excellent sense.

I always advise parents to let their firstborn youngster hold the new baby, feed it, even diaper it, if possible. I know the diaper may look a bit askew, but it's important to get the firstborn involved. If nothing else, let your firstborn go get the box of diapers for Mommy.

When the secondborn child comes home from the hospital, it will soon dawn on the firstborn that the "thing" is not temporary, that it is going to stay. Now it's doubly important to give the firstborn some special attention of his or her own. One good conversational tack is to talk to the firstborn about all the things the newborn *can't do.*

"[Baby's name] can't even catch a ball, he [or she] can't walk, can't talk, can't do anything."

Make a big thing about the newborn having to go to bed while the older child gets to stay up. ("You're three years old—you don't have to go to bed yet. You get to stay up late with Mommy and Daddy.") Dethronement is never a simple or easy matter. No matter how many precautions parents take, the firstborn can't help wondering, *Why this upstart? Wasn't I good enough?*[2]

Since the firstborn has had only adult models to learn from—Mom and Dad—it's no surprise that firstborn children tend to be much like "little adults." They tend to walk and talk earlier, and they have a larger vocabulary at a younger age. It's no surprise that later on—in high school, college, and adult life—honor societies often are glutted with firstborn children. Typically, parents enforce stricter rules and regulations with their firstborn. They want to do it right

with this first child, so they keep a tight rein. Together these influences tend to cause firstborns to be perfectionists who will face new situations and challenges with a great deal of caution. Firstborns don't like making mistakes. So with the arrival of a second child, they need some obvious reassurance that they remain as valued and loved as ever.[3]

As firstborns grow up, they may set great store by authority and power because of their "dethronement" experience. They may understand at a gut level the importance of rules and laws and play by them precisely in an effort to regain approval from the powers that be.[4]

In session 1 we looked at the story of the prodigal son in terms of how the father related to his wayward younger son. But the elder son also provides a classic example of the firstborn's struggles.

Divide into groups of four people each. Scan through Luke 15:11-24 to refresh your memory with the first half of the story. Then read more carefully verses 25 through 32, discussing the following questions.

1. At the beginning of the story, what demonstrates that the older brother was "playing by the rules?"

2. Where was the older brother when the younger brother returned? What does that demonstrate?

3. Why was the older brother so upset to find his father throwing a party when the younger brother returned?

4. What reassurances did the father give to the older son?

Taking the Squeeze Off the Middleborn

Every middleborn child was once the baby of the family but never the firstborn. In contrast to firstborns, middleborn children often have life a little bit easier. Mom and Dad are no longer so uptight. Nevertheless, if you'll recall the list of characteristics for describing middle children (session 2), it is riddled with contradictions. For example, middle children are usually sociable, friendly, and outgoing. But a lot of middle children also are characterized as loners, quiet, and shy. Many middle children take life in stride with a laid-back attitude. But under that blithe countenance is often a very sensitive child who can be as stubborn as an Arizona pack mule when riled.

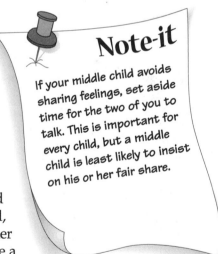

Note-it

If your middle child avoids sharing feelings, set aside time for the two of you to talk. This is important for every child, but a middle child is least likely to insist on his or her fair share.

It's harder to get a handle on the middle child than on anyone else in the family. The only child, the firstborn child, and the baby all stick out rather prominently. But the middle child blends in like a quail against the desert floor.

The same principles that apply to the secondborn are usually equally applicable to the middle child. Like secondborns, middle children follow their own version of Murphy's Law: *I'm going to live according to what I see just above me in the family. I'll size up the situation and then take the route that looks the best.*

If any generalization can be made about middle children, it is that they feel squeezed and/or dominated. It's important for parents to be extra aware that the middle child often feels as if "everyone is running my life." Not only does the

Note-it

Typically, the middle child feels squeezed by the brothers or sisters above and below. The middle child needs those moments when you ask for his or her opinion and let him or her choose.

middle child have a set of parents in authority over him, but he or she has a bossy older sibling right there also. And of course, just below the middle child is the baby of the family, who seems to be getting away with murder. The middle child feels trapped. He is too young for the privileges received by his older brother or sister, and he's too old to get away with the shenanigans that often are pulled by the baby in the family.

With these pressures from above and below, middle children wind up feeling like fifth wheels, misfits who have no say and no control. Everyone else seems to be making decisions while they are asked to sit, watch, and obey.[5] Some, of course, choose the route of rebellion—and then some!

Read Luke 10:38-42 and John 11:1-5; 12:1-8 about three siblings Jesus loved very dearly. From what you have learned about behavior typical of various birth orders, identify who you think was born first, second, and third, and why. Include all the clues you find.

- I think _____ was the firstborn because . . .

- I think _____ was born next because . . .

- I think _____ was the "baby" because . . .

Nudging the "Cub" to Grow Up

Lastborns seem to have some strange, mysterious power that softens parents who have been running a pretty tight ship with the other children. Maybe the parents have gotten tired; maybe they've gotten careless because now they think they "know the ropes" and can loosen up. Whatever it is, parents often look the other way when the lastborn skips chores and drives his or her older brothers and sisters crazy with pestering or what I call "setups." A "setup" is a particular lastborn skill that involves bugging an older sibling until he or she lashes out in anger, then running and screaming to Mommy for protection. If lastborns aren't getting away with murder, they are at least trying to manipulate, clown, entertain, or disturb somebody's peace.

Note-it

Be sure your lastborn does not get away with murder. Statistics show the lastborn is least likely to be disciplined and least likely to have to toe the mark the way the older children did.

Even if parents somehow manage to keep the family baby's antics under control, they can still be manipulated by that famous line: "I can't do it!" The plaintive cry for help is a great tool lastborns use to get parents (as well as older siblings) to snowplow the roads of life for them.

Be sure your lastborn has his fair share of responsibilities around the house. Lastborns often wind up with very little to do for two reasons: (1) They are masters at ducking out of the work that needs to be done, and (2) they are so little and "helpless," the rest of the family members decide it's easier to do it themselves.

Whiny lastborns are particularly adept at getting help with schoolwork. I have counseled several children whose seeming helplessness turned their homes into tutoring establishments right after the dishes were done each evening. It's one thing to encourage children with their homework and get them started; it's another to do it for them. Why not say, "No Little League unless you are cutting it at school," and be done with it?[6]

One thing I need to stress again is that no birth order profile fits every person. You may be a lastborn who wasn't spoiled at all. Or maybe your youngest child is hardly what you would call a manipulator. If anything, maybe your lastborn is the one being manipulated by the rest of the family. Ironically enough, while youngest children often are coddled and cuddled, they also can get more than their share of being cuffed and clobbered, especially by older brothers and sisters.

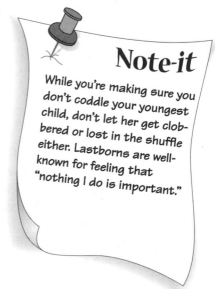

Note-it

While you're making sure you don't coddle your youngest child, don't let her get clobbered or lost in the shuffle either. Lastborns are well-known for feeling that "nothing I do is important."

Birth order specialists claim youngest children have difficulty with "information processing."[7] In other words, they seem to have trouble getting things straight. The older children always seem to be so smart—so authoritative and knowing. No matter that the older children are often totally incorrect in their dogmatic pronouncements to the baby of the family—the baby *perceives* they are right because they are so much bigger, stronger, and smarter.[8]

With their legendary "easy street" existence and their reputation for getting away with murder, lastborns nonetheless face several bumps in life that belie the claim that they have it made. As we've noted, lastborns may become too dependent and remain babies if they are coddled too much.

Note-it

Try to finish your lastborn's baby book before he's twenty-one. If necessary let other things go to catch up. Oh yes, try to pick out a nice firstborn for your lastborn to marry; it could make a great match!

Lastborns also can take a lot of abuse, pressure, resentment, and teasing from older brothers and sisters. Parents may sometimes think they need a crystal ball to figure out whether the baby of the family is really getting it in the neck or manipulatively working the system. I usually tell parents if they must err, let it be on the side of helping the baby of the family stand on his own two feet and cope, even if it means getting teased or intimidated on occasion. But a lot depends on age and size differences. After all, when you're the baby cub, getting teased is one thing—getting trampled is another.

One other hurdle for lastborns is that nothing they do is really original. Their older brothers or sisters have already learned to talk, read, tie shoes, and ride a bike. And let's face it: It is hard for Mom or Dad to get excited about the third or fourth lopsided pencil holder to be brought home from art class in the last five or ten years.

This is something every parent can be alert for with the lastborn: "Am I paying enough attention to little Harold's firsts in life? Yes, it's my third or fourth paperweight, but it's only his first. I should make as big a deal out of his firsts as anyone else's."[9]

At least be assured that your lastborn is well aware of his special slot in the family.

Responsibilities, Privileges, and Focused Attention

Assuming age-appropriate responsibilities in the family helps a child feel a part of the family. Unique privileges help a child feel special. Receiving focused attention—one-on-one time with just Mom or Dad—communicates unconditional love to a child. All three are useful in building healthy self-esteem and in defusing sibling rivalry.

Working together with your spouse or another parent of children approximately the same age as your own, identify three unique chores and three unique privileges that are currently appropriate for each child. Add a fourth chore and privilege that will *soon* be appropriate. Then identify one regular focused-attention activity *that the child will appreciate.* A focused-attention activity would be something that a child would especially like to do in which he or she is the focal point of the parent's attention.

Eldest child's name: _____ **Age:** ____

Responsibilities or Chores

    1.   3.

    2.   4.

Unique Privileges

    1.   3.

    2.   4.

Focused-Attention Activity _____

Middle child's name: _____ **Age:** ____

Responsibilities or Chores

    1.   3.

    2.   4.

Unique Privileges

    1.   3.

    2.   4.

Focused-Attention Activity _____

Youngest child's name: _____ **Age:** ____

Responsibilities or Chores

    1.   3.

    2.   4.

Unique Privileges

    1.   3.

    2.   4.

Focused-Attention Activity _____

Go back over your lists of chores and privileges. Underline any privileges you are granting your younger children at an earlier age than you did your firstborn. Circle any responsibilities you are postponing for them until a later age. Discuss your rationale with your partner. (Not all children are the same, so you may have a good reason. This is just to encourage a thoughtful approach.)

Come back together in the whole group for this last thought on keeping birth order in mind when trying to meet the particular needs of each child.

As she started her last year of high school, our middleborn daughter Krissy came home after the first few days with what I call the "long-jaws." Finally she burst out crying and said she wasn't ever going back to school; she wanted to transfer because she hated it. I waited until after dinner and found Krissy in her room, already tucked in bed and looking more glum than ever.

I sat down on the foot of the bed and asked, "What's wrong?"

"Nothing's wrong!" she snapped.

"Well, I'll just sit here for a couple of hours until maybe you'll want to talk."

Traces of a smile played around Krissy's mouth. She knew that the whole family was aware that she was upset; she'd made that plain enough when she'd gotten home from school. Finally she let it all out.

"I don't have any friends," she wailed. "Everybody I hung out with last year is in college, along with Holly. No one will even eat with me. I'm not going back to that school. I want to transfer right now!"

> **Note-it**
>
> Set up some privileges for your middle child, perhaps special time with Mom or Dad, going to a certain restaurant, or a non-hand-me-down new dress. The point is: This is the middle child's exclusive territory.

The plight of the middleborn—always behind the firstborn, feeling left out and left behind. Put that together with the fact that most of last year's friends had graduated, and this was one lonely senior.

I could have rushed in to reassure her. After all, Krissy is a naturally friendly, social type, and I knew she would make friends quickly if she gave it half a try. But I resisted the urge. First, Krissy needed someone to acknowledge her feelings.

"Nobody to eat with—that must be rough," I agreed.

"Everyone is mean and unfriendly. I want to transfer to another school."

"I can see why you would feel that way. I'd feel the same way myself."

"I'm not going back and that's final!"

I didn't point out the obvious: at another school she'd be even more of a stranger. But I did think it was time for a little friendly advice.

"Honey, I understand. I'd feel the same way you do. But I learned a long time ago that when you have trouble at school, you've got to face it. The longer you stay away, the worse it gets. Just go to school tomorrow. At lunch, find yourself a table—by yourself, and don't try to kiss up to the kids who are turning their backs on you. Just wait it out."

"Okay," Krissy said with a glower. "But I still want to transfer."

The next evening she mentioned matter-of-factly that a couple of kids had sat with her at lunch. By the end of the week, she had at least two good friends and several other kids she was hanging around with.

Meanwhile, Sande had called another private school in the Tucson area and learned that if Krissy truly did want to transfer, she could do so with no problem. We made that call not because we were permissively humoring Krissy's angry outburst, but because we wanted to show our middleborn that we respected her feelings. If the problem was really serious, maybe we needed to take her request seriously. But I had a hunch there would be no need to transfer. I was right.

> **Note-it**
>
> Be sure the family photo album has its share of pictures of your middle child. Don't let him fall victim to the stereotyped fate of seeing thousands of pictures of an older sister and only a few of him!

A few days later I stopped Krissy on the way out the door and said, "Mom made a few calls and found out you can transfer schools if you really want to."

"Transfer? Why would I want to transfer?" Krissy said sheepishly. "I've been going to the same school for four years. Everything's cool now, Dad, so don't worry."

Middleborns usually feel the squeeze, so taking Krissy seriously and giving her some room to maneuver gave her the space she needed to make her own choice: to stay at her school.[10]

Taking our children's birth order into account can help us to be sensitive to the particular needs of *all* our children.

Portions of this session were adapted from:

Leman, Dr. Kevin. *The New Birth Order Book* (chapters 11, 13, 14). Grand Rapids, Mich.: Revell, 1998.

Leman, Dr. Kevin. *Making Children Mind Without Losing Yours* (chapter 2). Grand Rapids, Mich.: Revell, 1984.

For further information, consider:

Leman, Dr. Kevin. *Growing Up Firstborn.* New York: Bantam Doubleday Dell Publishing Group, 1989.

Wilson, Bradford, and George Edington. *First Child, Second Child.* New York: McGraw-Hill, 1981.

NOTES

1. Adapted from Dr. Kevin Leman, *Making Children Mind Without Losing Yours* (Grand Rapids, Mich.: Revell, 1984), p. 32.
2. Adapted from Dr. Kevin Leman, *The Birth Order Book* (Grand Rapids, Mich.: Revell, 1985), p. 175 (Dell Mass Market paperback).
3. Adapted from Dr. Kevin Leman, *Making Children Mind Without Losing Yours*, p. 33.
4. Adapted from Dr. Kevin Leman, *The Birth Order Book*, pp. 224-225.
5. Leman, pp. 259-261.
6. Leman, pp. 272-273.
7. See Bradford Wilson and George Edington, *First Child, Second Child* (New York: McGraw-Hill, 1981), pp. 110-111, as referenced in Dr. Kevin Leman, *The Birth Order Book*, p. 280.
8. Adapted from Dr. Kevin Leman, *The Birth Order Book*, pp. 280-281.
9. Leman, pp. 283-284.
10. Adapted from Dr. Kevin Leman, *Bringing Up Kids Without Tearing Them Down* (Nashville, Tenn.: Nelson, 1995), pp. 197-199.

What You Say Is What You Get:
Encouragement Versus Praise

sk a group of "shorties" what their mom's or dad's favorite Bible verse is, and my guess is they'll roll their eyes and sigh, "Children, obey your parents. . . ."

Hey, why not? The first three verses of Ephesians 6 are the kind of "pithy truth" I like to clip out and put on the refrigerator door or pin to a child's pillowcase:

> Children, obey your parents; this is the right thing to do because God has placed them in authority over you. Honor your father and mother. This is the first of God's Ten Commandments that ends with a promise. And this is the promise: that if you honor your father and mother, yours will be a long life, full of blessing. (Ephesians 6:1-3, TLB)

"Children obey . . . God has placed [parents] in authority. . . . Honor your father and mother." Sounds good to me! (You too, right?) But before we wrap it up, let's not forget the fourth verse of that passage. In this verse the spotlight turns directly on parents and has a lot to say about the way we talk to our children and the effect that has on their spirits.

> And now a word to you parents. *Don't keep on scolding and nagging your children*, making them angry and resentful. Rather, bring them up with the loving discipline the Lord himself approves, *with suggestions and godly advice*. (Ephesians 6:4, TLB, emphasis added)

Whoops. This verse makes it pretty clear that God holds us parents responsible for *how* we use our authority, whether the way we communicate and discipline builds our children up or tears them down. If we "keep on scolding and nagging" (as *The Living Bible* paraphrases it), we end up with children who are "angry and resentful." In contrast, "loving discipline" includes "suggestions and godly advice" (instruction).

In other words, what we say is what we get.

Encouragement and Correction Versus Praise and Ridicule

There are ways of relating to our children that build them up and ways that tear them down. The difference can be as simple as whether you focus on your child's behavior or your child's character or personhood. Surprisingly, this is true whether the child has done something good or bad.

Encouragement and correction both address the child's behavior with positive results, whereas ridicule and praise can both undermine a child's sense of self.

Let me demonstrate how this works by asking a question. What do you think is the most important aspect of raising children: love, discipline, or encouragement?

You might pick *love* because nothing can be more important than love, right? Not necessarily. If all you try to do is love, love, love little Buford, you can wind up with a monster on your hands. Others might say *discipline*. After all, love without limits is no love at all. True enough, but the correct answer is *encouragement*. Rudolf Dreikurs, the father of logical consequences, wrote:

> Encouragement is more important than any other aspect of child raising. It is so important that the lack of it can be considered the basic cause for misbehavior. A misbehaving child is a discouraged child. Each child needs continuous encouragement as a plant needs water. He cannot grow and develop and gain a sense of belonging without encouragement.[1]

Note-it

Encouragement says, "It's great that something was done, and I appreciate it." Praise says, "You're great because you did something."

If you want to *discourage* your children, there are all kinds of weapons at your disposal: criticism, scolding, cutting remarks, doing everything for them (or doing it over because they aren't big enough, smart enough, or capable enough to do it right—according to *your* standards). But if you want to be a little more subtle as you discourage your kids, yet be every bit as effective, try praise.

Yes, I said *praise* discourages children. You may be thinking that Dr. Kevin Leman has really lost it this time. What's wrong with a little honest praise? Doesn't praise work with just about everyone? Isn't this a sound way to motivate children and build their self-image?

Ironically enough, many people think praising their children is just what they need. But in the long run, it can be very discouraging and damaging to a child's self-image. Perhaps you'll think I'm splitting semantic hairs, but I don't believe praise is the right thing to use on anyone, especially on kids. In short, I have come not to *praise* Buford, but to *encourage* him. Believe me, there is a world of difference.[2]

Note-it

Praise may trap you into comparing one child with another. True encouragement never makes these comparisons.

Responding to Positive Behavior

Why doesn't praise help? Let's look at an example. Picture the scene. We're on Any Street, Any Town, U.S.A. Mrs. Smith walks into her eleven-year-old son's room and discovers that he has cleaned it from stem to stern. She can actually see the rug, the top of the desk, and, wonder of wonders, the bed is made!

And to top it off, little Harlan is over in the corner, doing his homework.

"What a good boy!" Mom gushes. "Mommy didn't even have to ask you. You are the greatest. I love you so much for doing all this without even being told."

Now what's wrong with what Mom said? She told her son he was a good boy, that he was the greatest, and that she loved him a great deal. Don't all kids need to hear that?

Yes, our kids do need to hear that we love them and that we think highly of them. But in this situation, Mom isn't using the best terms because they're couched in the language of praise. And children can interpret praise any number of ways. When we use praise to stimulate kids into right or better behavior, their reactions can be anywhere from cynical (*So what?* or *Well, finally!*) all the way to the other end of the spectrum, which can leave them on the brink of panic (*Will I ever measure up again?*).

Note how Mom's praise centered on little Harlan rather than on *what he did*. In this case, his typical reaction to Mom's gusher of praise could well be that he would think to himself: *Hmmm, Mom loves me because I did my room and my homework. Would she love me as much if I didn't?* Or, to make matters worse, what if Harlan did this white tornado thing hoping that he would not get caught for cheating on his math test? He knows he is not a "good boy," and what will happen when Mom finds out?

Although praise seems innocent enough and even beneficial, only God is *worthy* of our praise. All others pay cash! Actually, praise affects a child's self-image in a drastic way. Children can easily get the impression that their personal worth depends on how they measure up to what Mom wants. When she praises them, their personal worth is up. But if their rooms are messy and she scolds them, their personal worth plummets.

Down the line, when little Harlan becomes an adult and gets out in the high-tech, fast-track world, his ability to cope and function well will depend a great deal on where he believes he stands as far as the opinions of others are concerned. When they tell him he's done well, his self-image goes up, and when he is criticized or ignored for doing something well, his self-image goes down. He will live on an emotional elevator.[3]

Imagine another scene where eight-year-old Edith kicks the winning goal in the last game of the soccer season. Dad runs around telling everyone that she is the greatest player on the team and might have a chance at a college scholarship. High praise for Edith, but not something she can live up to if this was the first goal she's ever kicked, and she knows that everyone else on the team is a lot better than she is.

On the other hand, Dad, Edith, and the whole team can be just as excited and proud if Dad's comments are words of encouragement that focus on the achievement and not on Edith. Who cares if it was just a lucky shot? Everyone can rejoice with Edith, and no one will be making rude comments behind her back (but within earshot) that she doesn't deserve her father's inflated claims.

Note-it

Ridicule attacks or belittles a child's self-image. It often begins with "Can't you ever . . . ?" or "How many times must I tell you . . . ?" and applies words like stupid, lazy, or irresponsible to the child.

Responding to Negative Behavior

The same dynamic occurs when we ridicule rather than correct our children for their negative behaviors. *Chicago Tribune* columnist Bob Greene pointed out the devastating impact of words like "Are you too stupid to do anything right?" said to one little boy. "Words like that can echo," noted Greene. In contrast, he reported how a teacher launched another boy into a career as a professional writer when she encouraged him with "This is good writing."[4] For good or ill, what we say to our children can echo for a lifetime.

Ridicule is destructive because it focuses criticism on the individual and his or her character. It becomes a label the child has trouble living down. This is very similar to how praise labels a child in ways that are hard to live up to. If the source of either ridicule or praise is a significant adult, it can be as permanent as a tattoo.

Now don't misunderstand me. I know little Casper needs your frequent intervention to change his wayward ways. However, the key is in *how* you do it. Correction is the preferred method. You correct the behavior; you do not label or belittle the child. To describe this process, the Bible uses many words that all focus on the behavior rather than the person: *correction* (Proverbs 15:32), *training* and *instruction*

(Ephesians 6:4), *teach* and *admonish* (Colossians 3:16), *exhort* (1 Timothy 5:1), and even *encourage* (2 Timothy 4:2).

Can you see the difference? Both praise and ridicule focus on the individual in a way that discourages and damages self-image. On the other hand, encouragement and correction focus on the behavior in ways that empower the child to try again (if it was good behavior) or free the child (to not be characterized by it) if it was negative behavior.

Of course the question always arises, "But I thought we were supposed to love our children unconditionally and *not* focus on their behavior." Saying "I love you" to your child frequently "just because"—when they come in from school, when they go to bed, or whenever—is quite different from saying, "Oh, Buford I love you so much," when Buford cleans his room. The latter discourages Buford because it feels conditional.

Parents do need to focus on behavior in the sense of encouraging right behavior or correcting wrong behavior, but not to focus on behavior in accepting their child and giving unconditional love.

 Divide into groups of three and number each group. Odd-numbered groups should follow the directions for act one, scenes one and two. Even-numbered groups should follow the directions for act two, scenes one and two. Each group should prepare to act out their role-plays for the whole group. See the guidelines in each scene.

Alternative: Mini-groups could write out their scene as a "case study" and read or report it to the whole group instead of doing a role-play.

For Odd-Numbered Groups

Act one, scene one: *Praise*
Write a short scene in which a narrator describes something a child did that was commendable. Follow this by a parent remarking on it to the child in terms of praise. Conclude with the child revealing (to the audience) how he or she interprets this praise and may act in the future because of it.

Act one, scene two: *Encouragement*
The narrator should review the situation that began scene one in which the child did something commendable. Follow this by a parent remarking on it to the child in terms of encouragement. Conclude with the child revealing (to the audience) how he or she interprets this encouragement and may act in the future because of it.

For Even-Numbered Groups

Act two, scene one: *Ridicule*
Write a short scene in which a narrator describes something a child did that was

wrong. Follow this by a parent ridiculing or belittling the child for the wrong. Conclude with the child revealing (to the audience) how he or she interprets this ridicule and may act in the future because of it.

Act two, scene two: *Correction*
The narrator should review the situation that began scene one in which the child did something wrong. Follow this by a parent correcting the child's behavior. Conclude with the child revealing (to the audience) how he or she interprets this correction and may act in the future because of it.

> Reconvene the whole group and invite the various groups to act out their scenes. Each group should be free to reverse the order of their scenes, giving the audience practice in distinguishing praise from encouragement and ridicule from correction.

The Problem with "Carrot-and-Stick" Discipline

Some parenting theories claim that if you reward positive behavior and punish negative behavior, children are quick to catch on and soon become little angels. Many parents have tried this "carrot-and-stick" system only to find that it doesn't work in the long run.[5] I've met parents who actually believe you should pay children for going potty! But let me ask you a question. Did you "go potty" today? Did anyone give you an M&M for going? I rest my case!

But why doesn't this system work?

Granted, rewards work with younger children for a while. Tell the typical three-year-old you will give him a lollipop if he does what you ask, and he will cooperate! Tell your twelve-year-old you will pay him five dollars if he'll clean up the backyard and ground him if he doesn't, and chances are he'll do the job. But sooner or later, every parent has the same question: Do I really want to bribe or threaten my children to do things they ought to do on their own? For example, just why should a twelve-year-old clean the backyard?

- He is a member of the household and the job needs doing.
- He will be paid five dollars for his trouble.
- He will become involved in the family and feel a responsibility toward helping it function.
- He wants to avoid being grounded.

Obviously, cleaning the backyard to pick up a five-dollar bill or avoid a grounding are much different motivations from the other two. After all, it isn't just Mom and Dad's home; it's the entire family's home. They *all* live there. When it comes to doing things around the home, it's preferable that the motivation comes from within, and I do not mean from within the pocketbook. The trouble with reward and punishment is that motivation always comes from without. If a reward/punishment system is the chief way you have of motivating your children, you are in danger of creating "carrot seekers" and "stick avoiders" who are always looking for a reward (carrot) every time they do something right, good, or noteworthy in life. They also develop resentment and hatred when wrongdoers don't get the stick.

I'm not saying that there aren't legitimate cases in which you might want to arrange a special project for which your child might be paid, but the far more common syndrome that I see in my counseling work is that parents often will get suckered into paying their children for just about everything they do around the home. If you are slipping into this kind of trap, now is the time to put a stop to it and have a talk about being willing to develop a lifestyle that centers more on self-discipline, humility, and good works without always expecting recognition in the form of cold, hard cash.

Similarly, I'm not saying that every discipline must grow out of some airtight logical or natural consequences. It's perfectly natural that Mother sometimes says to Tommy the Terror, "That's it! I've had it with you! Just go to your room." On the one hand, Tommy's rowdy play may not be a mortal sin, but Reality Discipline dictates that if Tommy doesn't learn at home that other people have their limits, he will face a much harsher confrontation with reality out in the world.

Note-it

Rewards, prizes, tokens, and lots of praise work for the short term, but they do not help children develop the maturity needed to cope with life.

Our confusion about the carrot-and-stick approach may have arisen in part because we do find the words "reward" and "punishment" used hundreds of times in the Bible. But do we attach the meaning to those words that the Bible intended? In his closing address to the children of Israel, Moses says, "See, I set before you today life and prosperity, death and destruction" (Deuteronomy 30:15). This is after he has rehearsed a long list of "blessings" (rewards) for their obedience to God's law and "curses" (punishments) for disobedience to it.

However, a closer examination reveals that most of the blessings can be understood as the *natural rewards* of obedience to God's wise laws. The curses are likewise the *natural* or *logical consequences* of disobedience to the most highly respected social code of conduct in history. While there are a few exceptions—such as God's promise to send or withhold seasonal rains relative to obedience or disobedience (see Deuteronomy 28:12,24)—it is usually possible to trace a direct tie between behavior and consequences, a Reality Discipline lesson in the way things work.

The Scripture reminds us that God's laws are perfect. They protect us; they make us wise. I'm no legalist, but God's laws *are* perfect, and they do protect us. God gave us families. God gave us parents to protect us. One meaning of the word *parent* is protector. I remember a fifteen-year-old girl who thought she had life so together she decided to run away and set off on her own, only to be found the very next morning strangled to death. What a tragedy!

Note-it

Be especially careful of praising firstborns, who are often perfectionists. With too much praise, they may develop a habit of not finishing what they start because they fear failure.

Often in our own parenting we have gotten lazy. We take shortcuts that are not related to reality and therefore do not represent "the loving discipline the Lord himself approves" (Ephesians 6:4, TLB). Our rewards are more like bribes—a lollipop *if* the child does what we ask. And our punishments are the first stick we can pick up to wallop the kid if he hesitates. When our children comply, we think we've produced delightful, obedient children, but we haven't. We're just building a time bomb. Thoughts are gathering in the child's mind that run something like this: *All right, Mom, you win this round, but I'll get even. I'm gonna get you back!*

We are teaching our children that because we—their parents—are bigger and stronger, we can push them around. We can force our will upon them. Because we—the parents—can get away with this, it reinforces the idea in our own minds that enforcing our will over theirs is the object of parenting. But that's not the goal. The object is, as Moses said, to prepare our children for "life and prosperity" not "death and destruction."

Divide into groups of about four people each and do the following Bible study.

- From Deuteronomy 30:11-20, read together Moses' charge to the children of Israel concerning the consequences connected to following God's law.

- Then review the Ten Commandments, the summary of God's law found in Deuteronomy 5:7-21.

- Suggest how each commandment can logically lead to life and prosperity or death and destruction depending on a person's obedience. (You may find it easier to begin with commandments five through ten and then return to one through four.)

1. You shall have no other gods before me.

    ■ Life and prosperity: ■ Death and destruction:

2. You shall not make for yourself an idol.

    ■ Life and prosperity: ■ Death and destruction:

3. You shall not misuse the name of the Lord your God.

    ■ Life and prosperity: ■ Death and destruction:

4. Observe the Sabbath day by keeping it holy.

    ■ Life and prosperity: ■ Death and destruction:

5. Honor your father and your mother.

    ■ Life and prosperity: ■ Death and destruction:

6. You shall not murder.

    ■ Life and prosperity: ■ Death and destruction:

7. You shall not commit adultery.

   ■ Life and prosperity: ■ Death and destruction:

8. You shall not steal.

   ■ Life and prosperity: ■ Death and destruction:

9. You shall not give false testimony.

   ■ Life and prosperity: ■ Death and destruction:

10. You shall not covet.

   ■ Life and prosperity: ■ Death and destruction:

Inconsistency and Hollow Threats: How to Raise a Yo-Yo

We've already talked about the three parenting styles: *authoritarian, permissive,* and *authoritative.* Authoritarian parents are always in control, never giving their children the freedom to make decisions or learn from their mistakes. Permissive parents provide very few limits under the guise of not wanting to "stifle" little Reggie's freedom to do as he pleases; basically, the children are in control of the family. As we've already seen, both of these extremes can create anger and resentment in children who either feel their needs and opinions don't count or "Mom and Dad must not really love me because they don't seem to care what I do."

But frankly, the most common scenario is what I call the "yo-yo syndrome." The children are constantly jerked up and down and back and forth between one approach and the other. On one hand are parents whose basic approach is permissive or at least soft on enforcing the rules because they want to make sure their children will like them. Finally, after being provoked beyond the limits of patience, the parents crack down with authoritarian fury. The word for this pendulum-like atmosphere is *inconsistency.*

On the other hand are parents whose basic approach is authoritarian and who intimidate their children into obeying the rules with threats full of fire and smoke. But the so-called consequences either are impossible for the parents to enforce ("If you don't quit fighting with your sister, you're going to be grounded to your room for a month!") or so improbable ("One more peep out of you and we're going to cut our vacation short and go home right now!") that even the kids know these are hollow threats and their parents won't follow through.

But before the rest of us who subscribe to an *authoritative* approach feel too smug, let's admit that even the best parents among us are inconsistent at times or make hollow threats. What tired parent hasn't been worn down by Tina the Toddler's whining and finally given in on that box of Choco-Wocos, breaking our own rule about no sweets just before supper? Or what embarrassed parent hasn't hissed unmentionable threats in a small ear that has been refusing to listen at Cousin Harry's wedding?

But remember the fourth verse in Ephesians 6? Children need consistency. They need to know what to expect from their parents. If we shoot off our mouths but are not prepared to follow through, kids end up being jerked around and feeling like yo-yos.

The good news is, the more you use Reality Discipline (which we will focus on in sessions 9 through 12), the more you automatically build the ABCs of self-esteem into your children's lives. (A) Because Reality Discipline combines unconditional love with reasonable limits, your children will feel *affirmed* and *accepted* despite being disciplined. (B) At the same time, your children will not only gain a sense of *belonging*, but they will feel worthy of being part of the family. They will know that they fit in. And finally, (C) because your children are held accountable for their actions, they will learn that they are *capable* and able to please you and themselves.

Divide into mini-groups of four (two couples or a couple with two single parents) and work together on the following matching exercise, which summarizes the last three sessions on building self-esteem in our children. If there are matches where you disagree (for example, whether it's "praise" or "encouragement," or "discipline" or "punishment"), discuss *why* you disagree. (Hint: there are more than two statements for some of the key words.)

Match the parent-to-child statements on the right with the type of communication on the left. (See the answer key on page 147 for my opinions.)

__ 1. Ridicule

__ 2. Discipline

__ 3. Hollow threat

__ 4. Punishment

__ 5. Acceptance

__ 6. Reward (appropriate)

__ 7. Bribe

__ 8. Reward (inappropriate)

__ 9. Encouragement

__ 10. Praise

__ 11. Belonging

a. "Once upon a time there was a special little girl named Holly, and she wasn't too tall, and she wasn't too short—she was just right!"

b. "Hey, Buddy! Daddy sure missed his little guy while he was away at work. But now I'm home and our family is together again."

c. "If I buy you that toy, will you promise not to ask Mommy for anything else?"

d. "If you take the trash out every day this week without complaining, I'll add two dollars to your allowance."

e. "You did a good job on your chores this morning. But I could use some extra help painting the fence this afternoon. I know this is your regular free time, but if you'd like to earn some money toward summer camp, I'll pay you $5 an hour for your time."

f. "You bought these earrings for me? You are such a wonderful daughter! You always know just the right thing to make Mommy happy. I sure do love you, Honey."

g. "Putting away the groceries while Mommy lay down was very thoughtful. I really appreciate it. Thanks."

h. "If you leave your bicycle lying in the driveway one more time, you won't be able to ride it for a week to help you remember to put it away where it belongs."

i. "Can't you ever put my tools away when you're through with them? That's it. Forget using the shop from now on. And forget going skating with your friends tonight, too!"

j. "If I hear one more peep out of you guys, I'm going to sew your mouths closed. Now shut up!"

k. "You call this cleaning up the kitchen? I should have known better than to expect a good job out of you. You never do anything right."

l. "Wow! I sure do like the bright colors you used in this painting. This picture makes me feel all sunny inside."

m. "You were late getting to the breakfast table three times this week. If you can't get up on time, you will need to go to bed fifteen minutes earlier. It's your choice."

n. "This is my oldest daughter, Penny. She's so smart, I'm sure she'll get accepted at Harvard."

o. "All right! Who started this fight? Never mind. It doesn't matter. You both lose your chance to go to Grandma's next week."

While still in your small group, share specific ways you can pray for one another—for instance: (a) wisdom to encourage a discouraged child; (b) God's help in understanding the difference between encouragement and praise, between correction and ridicule. Then pray around your small circle.

Answer key to matching exercise on page 146: 1 (k); 2 (h)(m); 3 (j); 4 (i)(o); 5 (a); 6 (e); 7 (c); 8 (d); 9 (g)(l); 10 (f)(n); 11 (b)

Portions of this session were adapted from:
Leman, Dr. Kevin. *Bringing Up Kids Without Tearing Them Down* (chapter 7). Nashville, Tenn.: Nelson, 1995.
Leman, Dr. Kevin. *Making Children Mind Without Losing Yours* (chapter 3). Grand Rapids, Mich.: Revell, 1984.

For further information, consider:
Briggs, Dorothy Corkille. *Your Child's Self-Esteem.* New York: Doubleday, 1975.
Dreikurs, Rudolf and Vicki Soltz. *Children: The Challenge.* New York: Hawthorne Books, 1964.
Leman, Dr. Kevin. *Keeping Your Family Together When the World Is Falling Apart.* Colorado Springs, Colo.: Focus on the Family, 1993.

NOTES
1. Rudolf Dreikurs and Vicki Soltz, *Children: The Challenge* (New York: Hawthorne Books, 1964), p. 36.
2. Preceding paragraphs adapted from Dr. Kevin Leman, *Bringing Up Kids Without Tearing Them Down,* pp. 162-163.
3. Leman, pp. 163-165.
4. Bob Greene, "Four Words that Changed a Life," *Chicago Tribune,* 10 November 1997. Reprinted in *Reader's Digest,* April 1998, p. 167.
5. This section loosely adapted from Dr. Kevin Leman, *Making Children Mind Without Losing Yours* (Grand Rapids, Mich.: Revell, 1984), pp. 48-55.

PART THREE

Reality Discipline

Why Children Misbehave

In desperation, a woman called our program one day and said, "You've gotta help me. My daughter is willfully disobedient."

"Uh, what do you mean?" I asked, intuitively wanting to get a better fix on this willfully disobedient girl before responding.

"Well," said the fit-to-be-tied mother, "I told her not to pull the books off the bookcase, but she looked right at me and pulled them down anyway."

Pulled them down? I thought. Hmm. "Down" must mean we're talking ankle-biter height or less. "So, what'd you do?" I asked.

"I spanked her good," she said.

That crackling sound she heard over the phone wasn't static. It was my brow crinkling with suspicion. "How old is she?"

"Nine months," said the almost weeping mother.

I almost dropped the phone in horror. "Wait a minute," I said. "What do you think nine-month-old children do for a living? They pull down books—and anything else they can reach. And in their free time, they put stuff in their mouths. That's what they do all day long. It's developmentally appropriate behavior."

You know, there are many times when we panic over our children's behavior because we don't understand why they are doing what they are doing. In this session we're going to look at some of the reasons children misbehave. It's my belief that all behaviors serve a purpose—positive or negative—and this is just as true for children as for adults. We'll know better how to respond if we understand what's motivating the behavior.

Like the woman who called me all in a dither about her "defiant" nine-month-old, parents sometimes mistake developmentally predictable behavior for misbehavior.

While age-appropriate behavior may need gentle shepherding, a parent doesn't need to panic and overreact. For instance, infants naturally put everything in their mouth, but as toddlers, they can be taught gradually that nonfood items are "yucky" and not intended for the mouth. Even in this teaching/learning process, some actions that look like defiance involve another natural process: the testing of boundaries.

When Mommy says, "No! Don't put the sand in your mouth," and little Edith looks right at Mommy and does it anyway, Edith may be less determined to disobey than to see if that word *no* still means the same thing it did yesterday. If Mommy goes ballistic, Edith may try it again just to see the fireworks—even though they were painful. Certainly Mommy needs to assure Edith that *no* means *no*, and at some point that response may include a consequence, but a calm response is the best way to stay on subject.

Actually, the wise parent minimizes using *no* before the age of two. Action is better than words. When an eighteen-month-old is doing something he or she shouldn't be doing, remove the child from the scene.

Here are a few typical behaviors many kids go through at different stages that sometimes confuse or worry parents that they may have a "troubled" child.

> ### Note-it
>
> Don't read too much into children's hedonistic, self-centered, experimental behavior before the age of three. They may know what "no" means, but their thoughts are only for the moment and only for themselves.

Behavior	Age(s)
Oral or anal fixations	0–2
Grabbing everything	0–2
Compulsive testing of *no*	2–3
Saying "No" to everything	2–3
Attachment to Teddy or "blankie"	1–6
Climbing up and jumping off	2–4
Biting	$1^1/_2$–$2^1/_2$
Fear of the dark	2–12
Hitting and kicking when angry	2–3
"Cruel" behavior like pulling cat's tail	1–2
Bossing others or being too submissive	2–5
Spilling everything	1–2
Blaming others and inanimate objects	3–4
Excluding others and tattling	3–7
Lying to avoid trouble	3–5
Bragging about possessions or feats	3–5
Sexual curiosity	$1^1/_2$–11
"I wanna do it myself!"	2–4
War or superhero games	3–4
Refusal to play with opposite sex	5–10

You may notice that in addition to children exploring themselves and the world around them, some of these behaviors begin to serve another purpose. *They gain attention!* Climbing up and jumping off is not only fun for its own sake, it also makes Daddy grin and Mommy gasp if they are watching. Getting attention becomes an increasingly important element in all behaviors—positive or negative.

Divide into groups of four or five people each, and then "tell tales" on yourselves. Use the following guidelines and questions to help you select a tale. Share your tale with your small group, giving, as well as you understand, the reason why you did such things.

---

1. Identify the age of your own child whose behavior troubles you most.

2. Think about your own childhood when you were *about that same age.* Remember a behavior that you did repeatedly that was outrageous, dangerous, exasperating to your parents or teachers, or in some way got you into trouble.

   ■ What kind of attention did you get for this behavior—positive or negative? From whom?

   ■ Was this behavior something that controlled your parents or others around you? (Something doesn't have to have been pleasant to you to have a controlling effect on others—for example, chronic bed-wetting.)

   ■ Did this behavior involve something over which you were so discouraged that you wanted to quit?

   ■ Did you ever set out to get even in a dangerous way with your parents, siblings, or others?

3. How did your parents (or others) respond?

4. How were you feeling at this time in your life?

5. What did this pattern lead to or how did it end?

This exercise is not to trivialize the anguish you may feel over some of your own children's troubling behaviors. But in some instances it may bring a calming perspective. It also may give some insight into why kids do some of the things they do. Of course, some of your own behavior may still be a mystery. That's okay. (At age eight, with the encouragement of my older brother, I used my trusty pellet gun to pick off my mom's prized Norwegian Christmas ornaments from the tree.)

 As a supplement to this session, view "Why Kids Misbehave and What to Do About It" from the video, *Bringing Up Kids Without Tearing Them Down*, © 1994 by Dallas Christian Video.

The Four Levels of Misbehavior

Psychiatrist Rudolf Dreikurs understood children about as well as anyone. He believed that when children misbehave, they may have any one of several goals in mind. Another way to classify these goals is to see them as levels of misbehavior, escalating from mildly annoying to severely irritating to downright dangerous and even deadly.[1]

1. *Attention-getter*. A child who says by his or her behavior that "I only count in life when I'm noticed or put other people in my service."

2. *Power-seeker*. A child who says, "I count only when I win, control, or dominate."

3. *Dropout*. This discouraged child withdraws to avoid pressure and expectations by appearing to be inadequate.

4. *Revengeful kid*. This child's goal is to strike back, to hurt other people—especially parents—because he or she feels hurt by life.

As we look at each of these motivations to misbehave, we will clearly see that self-image always plays a key role in what children do to annoy, control, or even hurt their parents.

Jesus' Disciples as a Family

There are ways that Jesus and His disciples illustrate many of the dynamics we see in our families. Therefore, we can learn from some of the disciples' typical behaviors as well as from how Jesus related to them.

 Gather in small groups of four people each. Have each person read one of the passages listed below. Each person should report on the events in their passage to their group. Then as a group discuss the following questions for each event.

- Peter walking on the water—Matthew 14:22-33

- Arguing over who was the greatest—Mark 9:33-37

- Disciples sleeping in Gethsemane—Mark 14:32-41

- Judas betrays Jesus—John 12:1-8; Matthew 26:14-16

1. Which level of misbehavior mentioned above (attention-getter, power-seeker, dropout, or revengeful kid) does this story represent?

2. Why was the person engaged in this behavior?

3. What was Jesus' response to this behavior?

It is important to note that comparing Jesus and His disciples to a family doesn't explain everything when it comes to Judas's betrayal. Jesus' tolerance of Judas's actions ("What you are about to do, do quickly"—John 13:26) stemmed from Jesus' larger purpose (to die for our sins—Mark 8:31) rather than from a failure to correct Judas's behavior as though he were a child.

Reconvene as a large group and consider the following four levels of misbehavior and some of the motivations behind why children employ them.

1. "Hey, Daddy, Watch Me!" The Positives and Negatives of Seeking Attention

- The child's goal is to get your attention.
- Your tendency is to react in annoyance.[2]

Because every child starts out in life with a natural desire to please you—the parent—you have a golden opportunity. Because children are going to seek your attention, you might as well do all you can to teach them how to be positive attention getters rather than negative ones. How you interact with your children as they seek your attention is a critical issue.

For one thing, go easy on the word *no*. I'm not saying you should never say "no," but I am suggesting that you use it sparingly. You'd be surprised how often you can change your natural inclination to say no by rephrasing your message to say: "That's good, but why not try it this way?" or "It would be better if we did this."

Two of the best strategies to encourage positive attention-getting in your children are these:

- Don't overreact to what your children say or do.
- Do show interest without putting on pressure.[3]

From the list below, place a plus before the positive attention-getting behaviors and a minus before the negative ones. Then for each behavior suggest an appropriate response, avoiding overreaction to negative behaviors or too much pressure for the positive ones. (I've suggested possible responses on page 165.)

___ Nine-year-old Chelsea insists on brushing her hair at the dinner table.	**Response:**
___ Roger, age three, dawdles and lags way behind when mother takes him shopping.	**Response:**

___ Six-year-old Lester tries to show all of the Sunday dinner guests the frog he just caught.	**Response:**
___ Barbara, age ten, has learned how to play a popular tune on the piano. After the twentieth time through—just after Daddy got home from work—it lost its charm.	**Response:**
___ Robert, age thirteen, has opinions about everything with the facts to back them up—from who played the best defense in last night's basketball game to the fact that there were two battles of Bull Run, with dates. And he'll tell you—whether you ask or not.	**Response:**

Pressure, expectations, or stress can cause of a lot of negative attention getting. When your children start seeking attention in negative ways, look for where they are being pressured, where life is closing in on them to give them stress and bad feelings about themselves. When this happens, they are headed over that fine line between attention getting and what I call power trips, using powerful behavior to control those around them, particularly parents.

2. A Power Trip Is Your Child's Reaction to You

- The child's goal is to show he or she is boss.
- Your tendency is to confront the defiance with anger.[4]

There is an invisible but very real line between negative attention getting and a power trip. Children cross that line when they decide they will *make* you pay attention to them on *their* terms.

It's important to remember, however, that children don't just "decide" to take a power trip. They are usually reacting to the way they're being treated by the parent. Children enjoy being led, but they don't like being driven. When parents use their authority without patience and understanding, children often will retaliate with powerful behavior. My friend and colleague, Dr. Grace Ketterman, said it best: "Show me a powerful child, and I'll show you a powerful parent!"

When parents use their authority without patience or understanding, they are taking their own kind of power trip, and often their children will retaliate with powerful behavior. They may talk sassy or have temper tantrums. But they also can take subtle power trips by turning "mother deaf" and just not hearing when being called to dinner or being reminded it's bedtime in five minutes. As Rudolf Dreikurs points out:

> [Children] resist our attempts to overpower them and show us their power instead. A vicious round develops in which parents attempt to assert themselves and the children declare war. They absolutely will not be dominated or coerced. All attempts to subdue them are futile. Children are by far more clever in a power contest. . . . the home becomes a battlefield. There is no cooperation and no harmony. Instead, there is anger and fury.[5]

In many families I deal with, children go on power trips because parents are inconsistent, vacillating between permissiveness and losing their temper, and becoming very harsh and authoritarian. In other cases, parents may be using power and over-control while believing they are "doing it all out of love" for their children.[6]

Note-it

Because of sheer exhaustion, single parents can be particularly vulnerable to power trips by their children. But remember, don't start habits you don't want to continue throughout your child's graduate school education!

Avoiding a power struggle does not mean simply giving up and permissively letting children do as they please. You are in authority. The key, however, is not to use your authority like a club or a leash. In general, everything depends on your *attitude*.

If your child's negative attention-getting or powerful behavior is really starting to get to you, what can you do?

When you know you're in a power struggle with your children, operate with the principle that you must "remove your sails from the children's wind." Children seeking a power struggle will huff and puff and try to get you involved in arguing and even screaming and shouting. Instead of being blown about by the wind, strike your sails. Don't engage in battle. Instead:

- Decelerate the conflict by speaking quietly but firmly.

- Don't argue with your children. Simply state what is needed and then remove yourself from the scene (or remove the child by putting him in another room).

- If the child is old enough and in any kind of receptive mood, sit down and talk reasonably, pointing out what you expect. Listen to your child's responses, coaching him to make "reasonable" requests, and then, without abandoning your "bottom line," allow him or her some latitude in making choices.

- With a child who displays powerful behavior by refusing to obey, simply give him or her a choice:

  "Do you want to go to bed under your own power, or do you want me to take you?"

  "Do you want to wear your sweater or your jacket?"

  "Do you want to stop complaining (stop crying, stop playing ball in the house, stop bugging your brother), or do you want to have a time-out in your room?"

This way you give the child a choice, but no matter what the child chooses, the child is obeying your wishes. Just remember, you don't want to let your child develop any habit you don't want to continue throughout you child's graduate school education.

 Divide into groups of four or five people each. Share situations in which you suspect a power struggle is going on between you and one of your children. Brainstorm ways to "strike your sail" while remaining in healthy authority. Use the tips listed above.

- My child, _____ , seems to be in a power struggle with me in the following way:

- One way I can "strike my sail" while remaining in healthy authority may be to . . .

3. Dropping Out: Completely Discouraged Derek

- The child's goal is to be left alone.
- Your reaction may be to give up.[7]

Children who display what has been called "complete inadequacy" are engaging in a subtle form of the power trip. They are acting out their discouragement in a very passive way. Instead of rebelling openly with angry retorts, bad language, fights, flagrant disobedience, and the like, children who feel totally inadequate simply give up.

Children who feel totally inadequate often have difficulty in school. They're behind in all subjects and flunking some of them. They play no sports and refuse to help at home. Mom has tried to get Discouraged Derek to help, but he is so clumsy or so slow, or does whatever he's asked to do so poorly that his parents have simply given up on him.

Discouraged Derek appears to have given up entirely. He is so out of it that he doesn't even want to try because this would take initiative and effort. He's finding that the best way he can cope with his lack of self-image and self-worth is to become helpless.

> **Note-it**
>
> When you encounter passive withdrawal, do not go on and on with lecturing, cajoling, or complaining about your burden. State what needs to be done, and spell out the consequences of noncompliance. Then be ready to act.

Also, he exaggerates any weakness, often complaining of not feeling good or of being tired. He is skilled at holding "pity parties" at which he is the guest of honor.

Completely discouraged children often appear stupid, but they are anything but stupid. What they are really doing is playing a very subtle game. Remember the old adage, "It is better to keep your mouth shut and be thought a fool than to open it and prove your detractors right"? Well, these children are putting it into practice. They are so afraid of failure that they'll do anything to stay away from having to try or make an effort. They think, *If I do anything or try anything, Mom will discover how worthless I am. I'd prefer that she just leave me alone.*

When children give up to this degree, the parents usually wind up saying the same thing: "I give up!" They decide there just isn't any point in asking little Derek to do anything because it will simply end in disaster and disappointment.

This, of course, is exactly what Derek wants. If he can convince Mom and Dad he is worthless, they will get off his back and stop hassling him. But what a price to pay for relieving stress in his life. Derek's self-image will remain puny unless he is encouraged and slowly brought out of his shell.[8] Sometimes "getting tough" with some loving Reality Discipline can help. Consider the following case.

Discouraged Derek

Derek had everyone—teachers and parents included—believing he was "simply not motivated." To demonstrate his broken spirit, he acted like he had a broken neck, letting his head flop, not caring about anything. "What should I do with this child?" complained his teacher to the principal.

"Send him home," the principal shrugged. "If he doesn't want to be here, it's not doing him any good."

A bit shocked, the teacher finally decided to give it a try. Next morning she went up to Derek, who was sprawled in his usual position, his head lolling on his desk. "All right, Derek," she said. "Come with me."

"Where are we goin'?" Derek asked.

"You're going home," she said. "Get your coat and hat."

Derek was shocked. Instantly his apathy turned to agitation. "What do you mean? Give me another chance! Please," he begged, and then he started to cry.

But the teacher stood her ground. "Here's a list of assignments," she said—and it was a long one. "You can come back when you have finished them all."

Surprisingly, Derek was back the next morning at eight-thirty, saying, "I have everything done."

According to the teacher, Derek made a 180-degree change in direction. Each day he walked into class with a smile on his face. No longer did he slouch in his seat; his head came up, his "broken neck" totally mended. He participated in class, raising his hand at every opportunity to answer questions or take part in discussion. Thereafter, he got good grades—mostly As and Bs—and was much happier.

4. Revenge: When Power Trips Get Serious

- The child's goal is to get even.
- Your reaction is to feel hurt.[9]

Beyond power trips and inadequate behavior are the children who seek revenge. Children on an active or passive power trip are not pleasant to deal with, but children with the goal of revenge can be downright scary. When a power struggle intensifies and escalates, it can cause children to seek revenge. Although their ultimate target is usually one or both parents, they may attack a sibling or possibly a friend in order to make their point.

For example, one boy of five went after his three-year-old brother while Mom and Dad were in other parts of the house. They came rushing when they heard the three-year-old's screams and found the older boy stabbing his little brother in the arm with a safety pin. The three-year-old got some punctures and the five-year-old got the attention he wanted—to be recognized as "really bad."

A child willing to stab his little brother in the arm with a safety pin again and again is in a very discouraged state of mind. Because he feels insignificant and unimportant, he is seeking revenge as a last resort. In all likelihood, little brother is outshining him and getting more attention from Mom and Dad than he is. He has finally become so discouraged that he resorts to something awful. He is convinced that nobody likes him, that he doesn't have any power, that he counts only if he can hurt other people as much as he feels they're hurting him.

What should Mom and Dad do with the five-year-old in this case? Punish him? If they do, his self-image will diminish even further, and his sense of self-worth will all but disappear. It has all but disappeared anyway. Also, the older boy will see punishment as revenge on him, and he will simply take more revenge in turn. The power struggle will become one of retaliation, answered by more retaliation.

What the parents must realize is that their five-year-old is unleashing his anger. He literally resents his little brother's presence in his life. What can his parents do?[10] Some helpful approaches would include the following:

- Remove the five-year-old from the situation, with possibly one parent attending to the needs of each child. Firmly but quietly tell the five-year-old he will not be allowed to hurt his little brother.

- Do not allow the children to be alone together until the underlying causes have been addressed.

- Take stock of how they are treating their oldest son. Does he have to go to bed at the same time as his "baby brother," or does he get to stay up at least another half-hour?

- Does the older boy have any special privileges because he's older? Do the parents occasionally make a "big thing" about his being the oldest in the family? Are the parents individually spending some positive time alone with the oldest son without baby brother in tow?

- Are the parents always saddling the older boy with "being in charge" of his baby brother—watching baby brother, doing things with baby brother when he'd rather be playing alone or with friends his own age? If so, the parents are creating a need in their oldest son to put distance between himself and "the thing" that has bugged him ever since he came home from the hospital.

- Is it possible the five-year-old is being abused by anyone?

Parents who detect any kind of revengeful behavior in their children should take it *very* seriously. Many children who reach a full-fledged revenge level do not recover. Our prisons are full of adults who are proof of this terrible fact. When children act out physically in a revengeful way, they may well need evaluation by a competent professional.

Not all children in a revengeful state of mind are beyond help, however. The level of the revengeful child's discouragement is a key. Youngsters who get in serious trouble at home or with the law are almost always extremely discouraged. They tell themselves, *I've been hurt, and therefore I have a right to hurt others.*

Though a child's goal in revengeful behavior may be to get even, the motivation is often the belief that he or she hasn't been heard or considered. Other measures may need to be taken when you confront revengeful behavior, but the first step is to *stop, look, and listen!* In fact, in some cases that is what the child's actions are screaming: "Stop, look, and listen to me!"

Taking Stock

 Go over the following questionnaire by yourself, then review it with your spouse or some other parent, preferably one who knows your child and can help evaluate your answers and form a plan.

1. Describe your child's behavior that you find most troublesome.

2. How would you evaluate this behavior?

> ❏ Age-typical behavior (proceed with questions 3 through 5)
> ❏ Attention-seeking behavior (proceed with questions 4 and 5)
> ❏ A power struggle (proceed with questions 4 through 6)
> ❏ Withdrawal to avoid pressure and expectations (proceed with questions 4, 7, and 8)
> ❏ Revengeful behavior (proceed with questions 4 and 9)

3. If it is age-typical behavior, how can you guide your child through this stage without making too much of it?

4. What kind of attention has your child received from you for this behavior so far?

5. How might you focus on the positive rather than the negative in relation to this behavior? How can you "catch him or her being good"?

6. How can you "strike your sail" while remaining in healthy authority?

7. In what ways have you lectured, cajoled, or complained? Describe them.

8. State what needs to be done, and detail the consequences of noncompliance.

9. Does the child's behavior represent a pattern for which you should seek professional help?

 Close with prayer for wisdom for all the parents. Also pray for all the children represented by the parents in the group.

Here are possible responses for the exercise on pages 156-157.	
_−_ Nine-year-old Chelsea insists on brushing her hair at the dinner table.	**Response:** Take the brush away or excuse little "Chelseakins" from dinner (with no snacks later).
_−_ Roger, age three, dawdles and lags way behind when mother takes him shopping.	**Response:** Pick him up and put him in the cart or you might try "losing him" without taking your eye off him. Let him discover that mommy is gone; with most dawdlers this will work.
_−_ Six-year-old Lester tries to show all of the Sunday dinner guests the frog he just caught.	**Response:** Personally, I think it's a great idea! I also found those Sunday dinners with cousin Herman a tad boring.
_+_ Barbara, age ten, has learned how to play a popular tune on the piano. After the twentieth time through—just after Daddy got home from work—it lost its charm.	**Response:** Although this is a great time to practice your Jimmy Stewart impersonation, it's best to say after about the 5th rendition, "Honey, Dad appreciates all your hard work. You're really learning. I'd like to hear more tomorrow afternoon."
_+_ Robert, age thirteen, has opinions about everything with the facts to back them up—from who played the best defense in last night's basketball game to the fact that there were two battles of Bull Run, with dates. And he'll tell you—whether you ask or not.	**Response:** "Robert, it's time to listen now, others need to be able to share as well." Away from others that evening talk to Robert about selfishness, politeness, and the need to dominate conversations. Robert obviously wants to be listened to and needs lots of attention.

Portions of this session were adapted from:
Leman, Dr. Kevin. *Bringing Up Kids Without Tearing Them Down* (chapter 5). Nashville, Tenn.: Nelson, 1995.

For further information, consider:
Dreikurs, Rudolf and Vicki Soltz. *Children: The Challenge*. NY: Hawthorne, 1964.
Elkind, David. *Understanding Your Child from Birth to Sixteen*. Boston: Allyn and Bacon, 1994.

NOTES

1. Dr. Kevin Leman, *Bringing Up Kids Without Tearing Them Down* (Nashville, Tenn.: Thomas Nelson Publishers, 1995), p. 106.
2. Adapted from M. L. Bullard, *Community Parent Teachers Education Centers*, Eugene and Corvalis, Oregon. Quoted by Vicki Soltz, *Study Group Leaders' Manual* (Chicago: Alfred Adler Institute, 1967), p. 78.
3. Adapted from *Bringing Up Kids . . .* , pp. 106-107.
4. Leman, p. 106.
5. Rudolf Dreikurs and Vicki Soltz, *Children: The Challenge* (New York: Hawthorne Books, 1964), p. 146.
6. Adapted from Dr. Kevin Leman, *Bringing Up Kids . . .*, pp. 111-113.
7. Leman, p. 106.
8. Adapted from Dr. Kevin Leman, *Bringing Up Kids . . .*, pp. 117-118.
9. Leman, p. 106.
10. Adapted from Dr. Kevin Leman, *Bringing Up Kids . . .*, pp. 121-122.

Combining the Power
of Love and Limits

I don't know how many of you waste your time watching some of the TV talk shows, but I am frequently an invited guest on a number of them. One day I was doing a two-part show with Sally Jessy Raphael—two hours back to back—on the subject of disciplining children. I was on a panel with a woman whose textbooks I had read in college and a psychologist whose name I have already repressed.

The three of us were sitting up on that stage like crows on a fence. We were about ten to twelve minutes into the show, and I had not yet said boo, even though this was my third or fourth show with Sally. So I started having this little conversation with myself (which we men are very good at, by the way), thinking, "Hey, Dr. Kevin Leman, you'd better jump in, or you're going to get left behind."

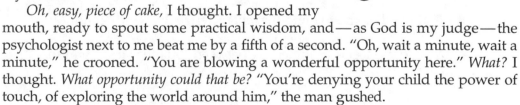

Just at that point Sally took a phone call from a man who had this question: "I've got a little guy who's three-and-a-half, and the bugger insists on playing with my $3,000 stereo, putting sticky hands all over the speakers, poking all the buttons, and twisting all the knobs. How do I get a three-and-a-half-year-old to stop playing with my stereo?"

Oh, easy, piece of cake, I thought. I opened my mouth, ready to spout some practical wisdom, and—as God is my judge—the psychologist next to me beat me by a fifth of a second. "Oh, wait a minute, wait a minute," he crooned. "You are blowing a wonderful opportunity here." *What?* I thought. *What opportunity could that be?* "You're denying your child the power of touch, of exploring the world around him," the man gushed.

Exploring the world around him? I thought the father was talking about his stereo. Maybe I hadn't heard the question right—but just then I glanced at the people in the audience sitting to my immediate right, and some of them were rolling their eyes.

Now, this probably has something to do with my birth order, I'm sure, but as the man continued to spew his permissiveness, I took my index finger and pointed it down my throat in Joan Rivers style, pantomiming "Aghhhhhhh!" while the man was talking. Sally Jessy just about fell off her stool, and the cameramen started cracking up. "Dr. Kevin Leman?" she cut in. "What did you just say?"

Jerking my thumb at the other guy, about one-fourth inch from his nose, I said, "Sally, I've got to tell you, I think this is a crock of psychobabble at its worst."

At that point, that tough New York audience erupted in spontaneous, raucous applause. They knew they were being duped. They knew instinctively that it's not going to scar a kid for life for a parent to tell a three-and-a-half-year-old "No! You may not play with the stereo," and let the child experience the consequences if he or she chooses to ignore the limits that have been set.

Children will misbehave, and parents must respond. But it's important not to take misbehavior personally and to consider the developmental age of the child when choosing how to respond. As parents navigate the path between permissiveness and authoritarianism, that's where Reality Discipline comes in. Reality Discipline is not in the business of punishing your child or making your love conditional on his or her good behavior, but rather on *training* your child with the combined power of love and limits.

Train Up a Child

Proverbs 22:6 reminds us, "Train a child in the way he should go, and when he is old he will not turn from it." Let's look at this nugget of biblical wisdom and see what it can tell us about Reality Discipline.

 Divide into groups of four to six persons and briefly discuss Proverbs 22:6, using the following questions as a guide.

1. "Train a child . . ."

- What words come to mind that characterize the word "train"?

- What do you feel is the difference between "training" and "punishment"?

2. "... in the way he should go ..."

- What "way" is being referred to here?

3. "... and when he is old he will not turn from it."

- What is meant by "when he is old"?

- What would cause a grown child to follow in the way he or she has been trained (as opposed to rebelling against it)?

 Regroup and share your findings. Add the following comments to your discussion.

Letting a child do as he or she pleases (permissiveness) or demanding compliance—or else! (authoritarianism)—is lazy parenting. *Training* a child takes time. It means putting thought and energy into teaching children acceptable behavior in a wide variety of social situations and preparing them for the realities of life.

The results are revealed when the parents aren't around. What makes a child behave responsibly when Mom or Dad isn't around to crack down? Perhaps it's fear of punishment; perhaps it's the child's conscience. But which has the potential for becoming "the way" a child will not turn from when he or she is an adult?

I believe that as you train your child with both love and limits, his or her conscience is developed in such a way that he or she is much more likely to behave properly when you aren't there. The best way to develop a sound conscience in your child is to teach accountability for one's actions and choices within a context of love, acceptance, and forgiveness for transgressions. You teach accountability by setting the guidelines—the rules or limits, if you please. It's important that our children understand what the limits are and why they are there. When they choose to violate the limits, it's up to us, the parents, to discipline our children swiftly and surely with consequences that are appropriate for the circumstances and the particular child.

Why? A more correct Hebrew translation of Proverbs 22:6 is: "Train up a child in his own way." This doesn't mean you let the child do whatever she wants (permissiveness). What it does mean is that

Note-it

You can't teach your children to be responsible; you give your children responsibility and let them learn how to handle it. As much as possible, give your children opportunities to solve their own problems.

every child is unique. He or she has a certain temperament, a certain way of reacting to situations, a certain kind of personality. Every child has his or her individual bent. Some children are more strong-willed or have a higher activity level and will need one kind of disciplinary measure in a given situation. A more passive child can and should be disciplined in a totally different way. Training a child in his own way means realizing your child is an individual and that each situation needs to be handled according to unique needs and temperament.

Reality Discipline gives you the kind of latitude you need to train your children in the way that is best for them.

Six Principles of Reality Discipline

The six principles of Reality Discipline are kind of like a Dagwood sandwich, with the "bread" (principles 1 and 6) of healthy parent/child relationships surrounding the "meat" (principles 2 through 5) of the nitty-gritty of effective discipline:

1. You are in healthy authority over your children.

2. You hold children accountable for their actions.

3. You let reality be the teacher.

4. You use actions, not words.

5. You stick to your guns.

6. You put relationships before rules.

Each of these principles is essential to the effectiveness of the others. Let's look at each of the principles one by one.

1. You Are in Healthy Authority over Your Children

We have already discussed this first principle in detail in session 4, but it deserves a quick review. Healthy authority rejects wrong behavior but always conveys love and acceptance to the child. In fact, when you use healthy discipline, you are giving children exactly what they want because children, despite what they may say and do, want the security of love *and* limits.

One of the major problems I see in many families, however, is parents who discipline their children but fail to communicate it in love. It is as if they think they can't do a good job of disciplining unless they are angry, cold, aloof, and severe. Only later, when they have cooled off, do they find it possible to be friendly and loving toward the children again.

The trouble is, children are relentless. They never stop testing the limits. Behind attention-getting behavior, which can turn into power struggles, under-achieving, or even seeking revenge (see session 9) is an even more basic goal: *finding out if you really do love them.* That's why the balance of love and limits is so important.

Balance is a key word when using Reality Dis-cipline. The child misbehaves, and you must deal with it. If you deal with it too permissively, the child will soon decide that he is running the house, but if you deal with it in a harsh, authoritarian man-ner, the child will feel that you are trampling him and bide his time until he can get back at you in one way or another. "Getting back" can run the gamut from being sassy or disobedient all the way to running away, getting pregnant, or com-mitting suicide. The tragedy that I see happen-ing repeatedly is rebellious children who literally destroy their lives as they seek to retaliate against parental authoritarianism.[1]

Note-it

- When teaching accounta-bility, the discipline should always fit the infraction.
- It is not your job to "make your kids happy all the time."
- Healthy authority rejects wrong behavior but always conveys love to the child.

It's important, parents, to keep in mind your long-range goal: helping your children become responsible people who know how to be self-disciplined and accountable for the choices they make—who can live with self-control and consideration for others. That's where the second principle of Reality Discipline comes in.

2. You Hold Children Accountable for Their Actions

I am convinced that the training ground for life ought to be the home. We must teach our children to be accountable for their actions and their decisions. In too many homes this isn't happening. Mom and Dad are always available to remind, coax, bribe, and push. Yes, maybe the chores do get done—eventually—but at what price?[2]

Part of the price is that Mom and Dad have to constantly nag the children, which Ephesians 6:4 clearly warns us not to do. But even more damaging is that through their constant nagging, coaxing, and bribing, parents are teaching their children to expect somebody else to always be there to push, motivate, and reward them for their behavior. But, of course, life isn't like that. We can give our children a great tool for living by teaching them to be accountable and responsible. As the old saying puts it, teach them to stand on their own two feet.

When I say that children "must be held accountable" for what they do, some par-ents mistakenly think I mean they must be punished. Again, let me underscore the fact that *Reality Discipline is not punishment.*[3] Rather, it is helping children learn that actions and choices have consequences. We do this in the safety of the home before they learn this the hard way in life, where they will face more serious consequences.

Divide into groups of four to six persons. Go over the situations below and brainstorm contrasting ways to respond.

SITUATION 1: *The Telephone Terror.* You're on the telephone and four-year-old Buford keeps pestering you—wanting your attention, of course. You try to remain calm, but Buford will not be denied. The racket gets so loud you can't hear the person on the other end of the line. What should you do?

    (a) punishment   (b) reality discipline

SITUATION 2: *The Big Spender.* You're in the supermarket checkout line and five-year-old Hortense begs, "Mommy, can I have some sugarless gum, pleeeeease?" Silently cursing all conniving supermarket managers who deliberately place the candy display where it is most likely to provoke parent/child battles, you'd like to put a stop to the "whiner wins" game right now. What should you do?

    (a) punishment   (b) reality discipline

SITUATION 3: *The Chore Chump.* Ten-year-old Harold more often than not forgets to take out the kitchen garbage each evening, and you usually have to nag him four or five times—okay, yell and scream—to get it done. What should you do?

    (a) punishment   (b) reality discipline

 Regroup and share some of your solutions with the large group. How do they compare with the following suggestions from the Dr. Kevin Leman School of Parenting?

SITUATION 1: *The Telephone Terror. The punishment solution:* You tell the caller you will be back in a moment, put down the phone, grab your four-year-old, turn him over your knee, give him three good whacks, and send him to his room. You have "taught him a lesson"—or have you? Now he's hurt, resentful, and not at all sure you love him. After all, all he wanted was you, and he didn't really understand what your phone call was about.

Reality Discipline: The answer is equally simple. It will take a little more effort, perhaps, but not that much. Again, tell your caller you will be back in a moment. Then take your little guy by the hand and lead him to another room in the house, or even outside if the weather is cooperative. Kindly but firmly tell your son, "I'm talking on the phone right now, and I can't play with you this very minute. As soon as I'm through, I'll come and help you with your puzzle" (or game, or book, or popping in a different video, or a snack). And then you leave your little boy to himself while you go back to your phone conversation. There has been no hitting, no angry hissing through clenched teeth—only eye-to-eye contact and a firm word from you about what you want your child to do.

Now I know what you're thinking. What if your four-year-old comes back to keep pestering Mom while she's still on the phone? The only reason your child will keep coming back to bug you is if he knows persistence pays off if he thinks that eventually Mommy will give in. But Mommy must not give in. Do not allow the child to remain while you try to pacify him and still carry on an intelligent conversation with the person calling. Remain patient, calm, but resolute. Ask the caller to wait, remove the child from the situation again, and let him know that he is accountable for his actions and that you will not tolerate rudeness or irresponsibility.

(A word of caution: If this is going to be a half-hour-long call, you might evaluate whether you should end the call after a reasonable time, give some focused attention to your child or redirect his play, and then call the person back.)

SITUATION 2: *The Big Spender. The punishment solution:* You lean close to Little Miss Hortense's ear and hiss, "You beg for gum one more time, young lady, and you're going to bed as soon as we get home" (or "I'll warm your bottom" or "you won't get to play with Freddie next door"). Hortense may (or may not) subside, depending on how convinced she is you mean business, but what about next time? After all, *sometimes* you buy her sugarless gum as a treat. How does she know whether this time or next time will be the magic number?

Reality Discipline: You look the child right in the eye and say, "Of course you can have some gum, Honey. Just use your allowance."

Hortense puckers up and wails, "But Mom, I spent all my allowance last Monday on the ice-cream truck."

"Oh, that's too bad," you say sympathetically. "Put the gum back, and when you get your next allowance, you can save some to get gum the next time we come to the supermarket."

Simple, isn't it? You put the solution for the child's problem right back in the child's lap. This solution presumes some understanding of how an allowance can be used as a strategic tool to encourage accountability for a child's choices (see next subsection).

SITUATION 3: *The Chore Chump. The punishment solution:* You tell Harold he's grounded all day Saturday (or loses some other privilege) because he didn't take out the trash three days this week and had to be reminded the other two days. He sulks and makes your life miserable all day Saturday, and he's still unclear on an essential fact: If he forgets to take the trash out only two days, or one, will he still be grounded? Or is three the magic number that gets him punished?

Reality Discipline: When you realize Harold has forgotten to take out the trash by the predetermined time, move in swiftly and calmly to deal with the situation. You negotiate with his younger brother Huey to take the garbage out. Is this imposing on little brother? Hardly. Little Huey gets part of Harold's allowance for his trouble!

Notice how Reality Discipline works in this case. Harold loses some of his allowance, but you haven't taken it away from him to "punish" him. You explain firmly but matter-of-factly that there is only so much money in the family budget, and when someone else must be hired to do something that's his responsibility, Harold must contribute part of his allowance to get the work done. If Harold is on the ball at all, he will soon learn that losing money due to forgetfulness, sloppiness, or rebelliousness is not a very wise choice. Not only that, but seeing his money going to his brother or sister will really hurt. Chances are good to excellent that Harold will make some drastic changes in his behavior and that he will get his chores completed on time!

In summary: Granted, it may take a little longer to hold children accountable for their actions, but it's worth it. Punishment may appear to get "faster results," but it doesn't help children develop the kind of conscience that will help them be responsible. They may learn to be fearful, wary, and even clever, obeying Mom or staying out of her way when she's around, but not being self-disciplined when she's out of sight. A healthy conscience comes from being held accountable and learning to follow the rules, because it is the most satisfactory way to operate in life, whether you're five or fifty.

3. You Let Reality Be the Teacher

One of the complaints I hear most from parents is, "How can I teach Johnny to be responsible?" But you don't *teach* children to be responsible; you *give* children responsibility and let them learn how to handle it through trial and error. When they make errors, natural or logical consequences come into play—*if you allow them to do so.* But if you're going to give children responsibility, you have to:

1. Give children age-appropriate choices, with the understanding that they can't simply change their minds if the choice doesn't work out.

2. Learn to use natural or logical consequences as teaching tools, not as weapons to punish. Instead of lecturing, badgering, or nagging, you let reality do the teaching when your children fail to carry out one of their responsibilities. Don't rush in to rescue them.

3. Back off and let children do things for themselves, even if what they do is not always perfect or up to your standards.[4] (Speaking of backing off, one of the best things a parent can do with a child is simply to stop asking questions. We set up the paradigm that we ask all the questions, and they learn to give really short answers—grunts, okay, fine, I dunno, and so on. When you always are asking the questions, you always are giving the message that you're not satisfied.)

Chores, Allowance, and Accountability

Two of the best strategies I know to help children become accountable and responsible are the use of chores and allowance. But how chores and allowance are given and used can make a vast difference in the behavior of your children. Here are a few suggestions.

- Every child should understand that, as a member of the family, he has certain chores and responsibilities he must do without any pay to help the family run more smoothly.
- Likewise, a child should get an allowance simply because she is a member of the family. The allowance should be seen as part of the family budget, a practical and effective way to give children the opportunity to begin to manage money.
- My own recommendation is that parents not make the allowance equivalent to "pay" for doing chores. Nonetheless, an allowance is not completely without conditions. For instance, if one child neglects his or her chores, another child can be paid to do them—an amount that comes out of the first child's allowance.
- Each child in the family should get a different amount of money for an allowance. The older the child, the more the allowance should be.
- The allowance should come to each child on a particular day of each week or each month, something children can look forward to on a regular basis.
- An allowance is something a child should be able to spend as he or she sees fit. If you give the child an allowance and then tell him how to spend it, the child learns nothing about handling money or accountability for the choices he makes.
- While I believe a child should be able to spend his or her allowance as he or she sees fit, the allowance also can be used as an opportunity to teach saving and stewardship. In our home, when a child wants to put some money in the bank, I encourage saving by matching that money dollar for dollar.
- We also teach and encourage our children the importance of giving some of our money back to God, but we leave it up to them how much.
- When a child wants a treat or a toy or designer jeans that aren't in the family budget, the child has a choice: to use his or her allowance, to save for what he or she wants, or to offer to pay the difference between what Mom has budgeted for basic clothing and the prize item Suzy wants.
- An allowance also teaches a child to be accountable when he or she is irresponsible—paying for that broken toy or window or lost library book.
- If a child uses his or her allowance irresponsibly and the money isn't there for chipping in for pizza with friends, the parents have a beautiful opportunity simply to let reality be the teacher and disciplinarian.

Stand up, stretch your muscles, and be ready to 'fess up! Select three spots in the room as Spot A, Spot B, and Spot C. Have someone read the following situations aloud and then move to the spot that describes how you would probably respond to these (or similar) situations.

SITUATION 1: Careless Carrie habitually forgets to take the lunch you packed for school.

>**SPOT A:** You trot down to the school with the forgotten lunch, and the next morning you remind her to take her lunch.

>**SPOT B:** You put the lunch in the refrigerator and let Carrie go hungry. (If someone at school loans her lunch money, she has to pay them back out of her allowance.)

>**SPOT C:** You immediately scold her when she walks in the door from school and say you hope she's learned her lesson.

SITUATION 2: In a fit of anger, little Hubert tears up one of his favorite toys.

>**SPOT A:** You give Hubert a big lecture, telling him how hard you work to pay for his toys and that you feel very hurt when he treats his Christmas toys so badly.

>**SPOT B:** You replace the toy, using a birthday or special event as an excuse.

>**SPOT C:** You say, "That's too bad. You loved that toy. If you'd like another one like it, you can save up and buy one out of your own allowance."

SITUATION 3: Billy has so much fun playing at the park that he forgets to look at his watch in order to come home by five o'clock, the time his father was to pick him up for the weekend with a very clear warning that he couldn't wait. When Billy finally races in at 5:45 and discovers that his father has gone on without him, he wails and begins to beg, "Can you take me over, Mom? Please! Just this once."

>**SPOT A:** You say, "Billy, I'm really sorry. I know you must be very disappointed, but your father told you he couldn't wait. I guess you'll have to wait until next weekend."

>**SPOT B:** You angrily reply that he is "late again" and send him off to bed without any supper.

>**SPOT C:** You scold Billy for being late but give him a ride over to his father's.

SITUATION 4: After doing homework, Lizzie watches her favorite TV show. But at bedtime, Lizzie suddenly remembers a report that's due the next day, using two forms of research on African birds. A zero might change her semester grade from B to C.

> **SPOT A:** You get upset at Lizzie and scold her angrily for her procrastination, but you give in and let her stay up late to do her report.

> **SPOT B:** Glad to see that Lizzie wants to keep her grade up, you rise to the occasion and tell her to look up information in the encyclopedia while you see what you can find on the Internet. If she writes the report, you will type it for her first thing in the morning.

> **SPOT C:** You sympathize with Lizzie that no report might lower her grade, but you remind her that bedtime is 9:30 on a school night and all homework is supposed to be done before any TV.

The idea behind letting reality be the teacher is to give children age-appropriate choices and let them decide if they want to be responsible enough to follow through. In the above situations, there is no need to lecture, harangue, or impose additional punishments just because the child doesn't appear remorseful. Give reality time to work. Reality provides its own natural consequence: going hungry at school; a broken favorite toy; no weekend with Dad; a lower grade for undone homework.

When you let reality be the teacher, you balance the need for order against making it okay to fail or make a mistake. Order and organization are important in the Reality Discipline home, but if children choose to disregard the need for an orderly approach to life, they are not ridiculed and punished. They simply learn the hard way through personal experience that irresponsibility or poor choices have unpleasant consequences. But because Mom and Dad let reality be the teacher, kids also learn that it's okay to make mistakes, and they can learn from their failures.[5]

But natural consequences are not always "built in" to a situation. Sometimes parents have to take action to help children experience the consequences of their choices. That's where the next principle of Reality Discipline comes in.

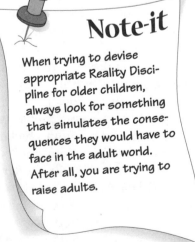

Note-it

When trying to devise appropriate Reality Discipline for older children, always look for something that simulates the consequences they would have to face in the adult world. After all, you are trying to raise adults.

4. You Use Actions, Not Words

We all know the cliché, "Actions speak louder than words," but it remains as true as ever, especially in regard to child rearing. Our kids don't always pay attention to what we say—especially if it's not backed up by action. So I tell parents: "Sometimes you have to pull the rug out and let the little buzzards tumble!"

While it's important to speak in a friendly and matter-of-fact way to your children when using Reality Discipline, it's equally important that you keep arguing and debating to a minimum. The longer you dialogue with children about why something is being done or why something is fair or not fair, the more you enter into the power struggle conflicts described in the last session.

You have a child who fusses about wearing his seat belt? Or won't quit pestering his sibling? Don't argue about it. Simply pull over, STOP THE CAR, and say that the car isn't moving again until all seat belts are fastened or the fighting stops.

Kids love to act up in the car. They know Mom or Dad is driving and can't do much about it—except yell, in which case Festus and Felicia quiet down for about thirty seconds, and then it starts all over again.

> **Note-it**
>
> A key to Reality Discipline is always to keep responsibility squarely on the shoulders of the child. Reality Discipline is short on lectures and harangues, quick to take action.

You will get much better results if you simply act swiftly and decisively with a minimum of unnecessary conversation. They won't stop fighting? Turn the car around and take them home, even if they miss the soccer game or Bible Whiz Kids. Let them know they have a choice: They can choose to let Mom drive them peacefully to their activities, or they can choose not to be driven. The first time you abort a trip to somewhere they want to go will probably be the last time you have to do it.

You aren't trying to hurt the "little buzzards." Your goal is to communicate the consequences of ignoring reality. If the reality of irresponsible actions or poor choices is not naturally built into the situation, the parent needs to help "pull the rug out."

This is what I suggested to Todd's parents.[6] Todd was the baby of the family and a fussy eater. He liked potatoes mashed, but not boiled or baked. He liked his pancakes spread out on the plate, not stacked on top of one another. Naturally, there were all kinds of hassles at meals. After learning something about my ideas on Reality Discipline, Mom went home and made fried chicken for dinner. Todd took one look, stuck out his lip and said, "I don't like chicken."

Mom was puzzled because Todd had eaten two helpings of chicken last week, but she didn't go into her usual routine of, "Honey, of course you like chicken. Besides, if you eat your chicken you'll get your special strawberry shortcake for dessert." Instead, Mom quietly picked up Todd's plate, went over to the kitchen sink, and with a flick of the wrist, Todd's dinner was over.

Todd was stunned. He probably thought, *Mom has flipped! She's always telling me how much food costs, and she just threw my dinner in the garbage!*

Was Mom's action too severe? Should she have tried to reason with him? She had already tried that many times. No, I believe her action was correct. It is always the perfect disciplinary action with kids who won't eat what is put before them. It actually gives them a choice: to eat or not to eat. And it holds them accountable if they choose to be picky or fussy because the final pull on the rug is that there are no snacks, no treats, nothing at bedtime. They are free to leave the table. They can play, do their homework, do whatever their usual routine is, and there will be no punishment. But there is discipline—the discipline of being accountable for the choices they make.

In Todd's case, his mother recalls that he ate one of the biggest breakfasts of his life the next morning. And life improved immeasurably in that family.

At our house, Sande and I try to split up the rug-pulling chores as much as possible. We have been pulling the rug and letting Holly, Krissy, Kevin, Hannah, and Lauren tumble all their lives, and our little buzzards don't appear to be any worse for the wear. The reason? We love them with all that is in us, and they know it!

We don't pull the rug out as a form of punishment or vengeance. We don't pull the rug out to dominate our children or take parental ego trips. We pull the rug with love (and sometimes it takes tremendous commitment to do it because it hurts). It would be easier to just hug them, cuddle them, and coddle them, but this would not teach them the accountability and responsibility they need to face life later. There will be a day when our kids are too big for a lot of hugging and cuddling. And that is when our love will still be touching their lives in a tangible sense as they go about the task of being accountable and responsible adults.

Working individually, describe at least one discipline problem for each of your children where you have been using words instead of action. Then share the problems you identified with your spouse. Do the two of you approach the same problem differently? Identify the difference. (If you are a divorced parent and approach discipline differently than your "ex," share with another parent in a similar situation and brainstorm ways to bridge the gap.)

Firstborn   **Middleborn**   **Lastborn**

5. You Stick to Your Guns

In a very real sense, the entire Reality Discipline system rides on this principle. It will do no good to put your children in a place where they are accountable and let reality do the teaching if you step in at the last second to bail them out and let them off the hook.

Granted, it is hard to stick to your guns. Sometimes it is downright painful for you as well as for the children. What mom or dad wants to see a hungry child have to wait clear till the next meal or go to bed without dinner? What parent is really eager to let a child go to school without homework done—a reflection not only on the child but on the parent as well? And what parent enjoys seeing a child lose hard-earned money?

Unless you allow your children to suffer the pain involved in the consequences for being irresponsible, they will never learn accountability. You will simply go right back to the same inconsistent seesaw of giving in for a while on one hand (being permissive) and then cracking down on the other (authoritarian). How can you psych yourself up so you are able to stick to your guns without feeling like a heartless ogre?

First, always look at the big picture. What will your child be like down the line when he or she is an adult? It may be hard to enforce Reality Discipline at the moment, but remember that you're doing it because you don't want your kids growing up and throwing temper tantrums in front of professors or employers some day.

Luke 16:10 says, "Whoever can be trusted with very little can also be trusted with much." You are training your children to be accountable for the bigger responsibilities of life by being responsible in smaller things. If your teenager is irresponsible at home or in school, there is no way he or she should be allowed to drive the family car (or any other car, for that matter). Any parent who allows children to grow up without developing a responsible attitude is asking for something terrible to happen in the future.

Second, remind yourself that your goal as a parent is not to solve every problem for your children immediately. Children should be learning how to solve their own problems. There is no instant maturity, no instant happiness. In fact, it is a rule of life that we cannot be happy all of the time. I run into so many parents who feel that their mission in life is to "make their kids happy." The truth is, Reality Discipline may sometimes bring unhappiness for a brief period, but it helps children develop the maturity that leads to true happiness and satisfactory living later on.

On the walls of gyms and workout centers across the world you will find the slogan: No Pain, No Gain. This is equally true for the home. If there is to be real emotional growth and development, there has to be some pain. Parents must prepare their children to deal with the reality that in life, we don't always get what we want. The home should be a proving ground for this very profound truth. And what better place for children to learn about reality than in the protective boundaries of their own family, where there is love, concern, and support?[7]

This leads to the last principle of our Dagwood sandwich.

Note-it

Reality Discipline will not work unless you stick to your guns and make your child be accountable, even if it is somewhat painful for both of you.

6. You Put Relationships Before Rules

Josh McDowell, who speaks to thousands of young people on college and high school campuses every year, has a favorite saying: "Rules without relationships lead to rebellion." He's right. Invoking limits without communicating love not only erodes a child's sense of self-worth, it drives a bigger and bigger wedge between the two of you.[8]

Most of you will say, "But of course I love my children!" But sometimes even the best relationships become strained under the onslaught of daily power struggles and worry about all the negative influences on your children from school, peers, and the media. You love your kids—but do you have a *relationship* with them?

In session 12 we'll focus on keeping a healthy relationship with our kids—including mutual respect, grace and forgiveness, enjoying our kids, and keeping our sense of humor.

 With your spouse, get together in groups of four to six. Single parents can either group together or pair up and join a group of two couples. (If possible, each couple or single parent should have at least one other couple or single parent in their group.) Follow the guidelines below.

Share and Pray:

- Take turns sharing the discipline problems you identified earlier with each of your children.

- Brainstorm and share ideas with each other of ways to hold your children accountable for their behavior. How can you let reality be the teacher? Use actions instead of words? Pull the rug out and let the kids tumble? Stick to your guns?

- Discuss how you can handle situations when your spouse or ex-spouse disciplines very differently from your preferred approach.

- Commit yourselves to working on at least one new way to use Reality Discipline in your home in the coming week.

- Pray for each other asking God to give you the strength to use the power of love and limits in your home.

Portions of this session were adapted from:

Leman, Dr. Kevin. *Bringing Up Kids Without Tearing Them Down* (chapter 6). Nashville, Tenn.: Nelson, 1995.

Leman, Dr. Kevin. *Making Children Mind Without Losing Yours* (chapters 3 and 4). Grand Rapids, Mich.: Revell, 1984.

NOTES

1. Adapted from Dr. Kevin Leman, *Making Children Mind Without Losing Yours* (Grand Rapids, Mich.: Revell, 1984), p. 110.
2. Adapted from Dr. Kevin Leman, *Making Children Mind . . .*, p. 63.
3. Adapted from Dr. Kevin Leman, *Bringing Up Kids Without Tearing Them Down* (Nashville, Tenn.: Nelson, 1995), p. 138.
4. Adapted from Dr. Kevin Leman, *Bringing Up Kids . . .*, pp. 145-146.
5. Adapted from Dr. Kevin Leman, *Bringing Up Kids . . .*, pp. 147-148.
6. Adapted from *Making Children Mind . . .*, pp. 81-83.
7. Adapted from Dr. Kevin Leman, *Bringing Up Kids . . .*, pp. 153-155.
8. Adapted from Dr. Kevin Leman, *Bringing Up Kids . . .*, p. 155.

Reality Discipline
for Real Families

Parenting preschoolers is the nearest thing to "Double Jeopardy" that I know of. After all, a child's personality, character, and emotional makeup are pretty much formed by ages five to seven. Also, moms and dads of firstborn preschoolers are new to the parenting game, learning by trial and error, which jacks up the stress level even higher. I have a special concern for all the firstborns of this world. Sometimes I think it's a miracle that they survive.

After "learning on the first child," parents often decide to have one or two more—only to get a rude awakening. Children are different! What worked with the first child doesn't necessarily work with middleborn or lastborn. Meanwhile, their firstborn is now beyond the preschool "wonder years" and has stumbled into the "blunder years," learning to cope with an ever-widening world of school, friends, and activities.

And then, the teen years arrive. If you think the teen years are hard on parents, try being the teenager! It's a turbulent time when everything is exaggerated. A simple zit becomes Mt. Saint Helens. Your teen would *die* before being seen in public in anything except a certain brand of athletic shoes. An embarrassing moment in front of friends means "My life is *over!*" Teenagers live for now. Yesterday is ancient history, next week is the far distant future. Coping with being who they are right now, this minute—unsure, insecure, living in mortal fear of the censure of their peers—is enough of a challenge.

Can Reality Discipline really help parents shepherd their children through all these different ages and stages toward becoming confident, responsible adults? I believe it can, but of course it must be applied in age-appropriate ways. Before we look at how to use Reality Discipline at different ages and stages, here are a few things to keep in mind:

1. Remember that all (mis)behavior has a purpose. Before reacting to a situation, practice *active listening* to your child for careful assessment of the situation.

2. When a child has strong feelings, *respond to his or her feelings* in a way that encourages, not discourages.

3. When you have strong feelings, *direct your feelings or actions toward the (mis)behavior,* not the child.

When discipline is called for:

1. Put the responsibility for solving the problem *squarely on the child's shoulders.*

2. If possible, give the child a *choice.*

3. When holding a child accountable, *discipline should always fit the (mis)behavior* as much as possible.

Group yourselves according to the age of your oldest child (or child that is the most challenging to you): preschooler, "middler" (ages six to twelve), or teenager. As small groups, go through the following examples of Reality Discipline for your age group. After *each* type of example, share similar experiences with your own child. Keeping in mind the guidelines above, help each other brainstorm possible Reality Discipline responses. Spend the majority of this session in these small groups.

Reality Discipline for Parents of Preschoolers

Temper Tantrums

Tina, age three, throws a temper tantrum right in the middle of the living room in front of guests. At a time like this, action is always better than words. Mom does not try to reason with her little screamer, but simply picks her up and removes her from the scene so she cannot get the attention she's seeking in a negative way. Mom leaves her in her room, shuts the door, and goes back to her guests. When Mom hears that Tina has quieted down some, she can go to Tina's room and tell her that when she's ready to return quietly, she may do so. Leaving the choice to Tina is better than Mom assuming Tina is ready to return.

One time my preschooler threw a tantrum in the middle of the mall. Muttering, "Honestly! Some people's kids!" I stepped right over her and kept on walking.

She looked up in astonishment, ran after me, and threw herself down in another tantrum. I stepped over her again, keeping her in sight out of the corner of my eye. Again she ran after me, but this time she figured out the tantrum wasn't working and gave up.

Five-year-old Terry plays beautifully at a friend's house for the afternoon, but when Mom comes to pick him up, he throws a fit. Mom doesn't negotiate, bribe, or argue. She simply picks up her child (literally, if necessary) and leaves immediately. But the next time Terry wants to play with this friend, he is told no and reminded of the scene he caused. "That kind of behavior will not be tolerated." Even though he pleads and promises to be good, let him miss one play time. The next time he asks, Mom says she is willing to try again, but she expects better behavior when she comes to pick him up. If Terry handles himself better this time, Mom can say, "You did a good job leaving when I came to pick you up today. I think you can go play with your friend again soon."

(If you are a single parent and a similar tantrum occurs when you arrive to pick up your child from your ex-spouse, the Reality Discipline suggested above may not be possible without prior arrangement because of court-ordered visitation guarantees. Therefore you might need to come up with another response.)

 What temper tantrums have you suffered? What did you do? What happened? Share with the group. Brainstorm Reality Discipline responses.

Bedtime

Children—particularly the very young—frequently have fears, and these fears tend to center around bedtime: fear of the dark, fear of being left alone, fear of monsters under the bed. It's also true that children love to manipulate Mommy and Daddy so they can stay up longer and have company by calling out, asking for a drink (and another, and another), and—here's the killer—saying they have to go to the bathroom. What parent wants to risk a wet bed?

Here are a few bedtime tips to minimize bedtime hassles:

- Don't let your child watch violent or scary TV shows before going to bed.

- Make going to bed a special time; avoid using going to bed as punishment.

- Establish a consistent routine. Brushing teeth, going to the toilet, reading one or two stories, singing one or two songs, tucking in, praying together. Don't rush this time.

- A nightlight or a light in the hall may take care of fears of the dark.

- Occasionally, if a child seems wound up or not sleepy, you might allow the child to "look at books" in bed or listen to a story tape until she gets sleepy.

- But once your child is in bed with all needs cared for, the door stays shut. Do not return if your child cries or screams.

- If your child keeps coming out for company, immediately return the child to his room and leave him there with minimal interaction.

- For an older child (four or five) who is not cooperating, tell him that if he doesn't settle down, he will have to go to bed half an hour earlier the next night. Add fifteen minutes for every time he comes out. Then be sure you follow through!

 Do you have bedtime hassles with your preschooler? Brainstorm ways to respond using Reality Discipline with your small group.

Mealtimes

Even young children can be given reasonable choices, which help them learn to be accountable. Mom asks little Tommy if he'd like a peanut butter sandwich or a tuna sandwich for lunch. Tommy chooses peanut butter, and Mom makes herself a tuna sandwich. After one bite of his PB&J, Tommy changes his mind and decides he wants tuna after all. What should Mommy do? Give Tommy her tuna and eat his peanut butter? Make another tuna sandwich and wrap up the peanut butter for another day? Coax Tommy to eat the peanut butter sandwich by playing "airplane" with it?

No, Mom gave Tommy a choice, but not the option to keep changing his choice. At this point she says, "You can eat your peanut butter, or you can get down from the table, and lunch is over." Quite possibly Tommy will get down and run off to play. *Now comes reality for both Tommy and Mom:* before dinner—possibly *well* before dinner—Tommy will be back whining about how hungry he is. This is a crucial moment. Mom may feel a pang of guilt, but she must pray for strength and not give in. She has to let Tommy know that making decisions is important. "Yes, I'll bet you're hungry. Since you didn't eat your lunch, you must be starved! Well, you're in luck. We're going to have dinner in about two hours when Daddy gets home. Now run along and play."

 Got picky eaters at your table? What works (and doesn't work) at your house? Brainstorm Reality Discipline responses with the small group.

Picking Up Toys

I recall working with a mother whose four-year-old used whining, crying, and fussing as a way of keeping himself in control of situations at home. One afternoon, Mom had a dentist appointment, so she asked Jimmy to pick up his toys before they left the house. But little Jimmy whined, "They're too heavy."

Mom left the toys on the floor and took the child with her to the dentist. On the way home, Jimmy began working on Mom for an ice cream treat. But as they drove by the ice cream store, Mom said quietly, "Honey, you can't have a treat today. You still have work left to do at home. You know our rule: work before play or treats."

When they arrived home, there were the toys, lying where they had been left. Jimmy got the message. He picked up his toys and put them away. But if he still didn't want to pick up his toys, Mom could have invoked Reality Discipline in further ways by not allowing him to do anything until his chore was satisfactorily completed: no playing, no television, no snacks or treats. Reality Discipline stresses order, that A (the responsibility) comes before B (the privilege).[1]

Another mother complained that her three-year-old daughter always said "Why?" when asked to do something. After asking about three times, the mother would reach for the paddle, at which point the child would immediately jump up and pick up the toys (or whatever) to avoid a spanking. I told this mother that she was training her child beautifully to ignore her until she reached for the paddle, creating a "powerful little buzzard." I told her to ask just once, allow an appropriate time for compliance, then take her daughter by the hand, sit down by the toys and say, "Let's pick up the toys now." Keep in mind that with three-year-olds, you must take the time to train them. Mom and Dad need to make a commitment to ask just once, and then take action.

> Who picks up toys at your house? How many ways does your preschooler invent to get out of the chore? Brainstorm Reality Discipline responses.

Stealing

A mother wrote to me and said, "The other day my five-year-old took a Tootsie Pop from the grocery store and I didn't notice until we got to the car. I took her back in the store, made her apologize to the clerk, and then paid for the pop. Because I felt facing the clerk was punishment enough, I let her keep the Tootsie Pop (which

Note-it

Even young children can be given reasonable choices which help them learn to be accountable. Blue shorts or red shorts, game or story, milk or juice—but not the option to keep changing their choice.

was now paid for) and eat it on the way home. But my husband thinks I should have thrown the Tootsie Pop away. Is he right?"

Absolutely! As it is, the child was eventually rewarded for stealing by getting to eat the candy. Not only should this mother have led her daughter to a trash basket and guided her to throw away the pop, but if the child got any kind of allowance, she should pay her mother back for the candy. Even though preschoolers (especially toddlers) may not see an incident like this—or taking a toy from a friend's house without asking—as "stealing," they must be helped to see that it is wrong and will never be tolerated.[2]

 Uh-oh. Do you have any "sticky fingers" at your house? With your small group, come up with Reality Discipline for specific situations.

Forgetting

Another mom wrote: "I thought I had my three-year-old fully potty trained (he didn't really learn until he was almost three), but lately he's been coming in the house from play with wet pants. He tells me he 'forgets' to come in and go to the bathroom. I've tried spanking him and making him stay in his room, but he still continues to 'forget.' Any ideas?"

First of all, spanking is totally the wrong response for potty training accidents or forgetting or any other "childish" misbehavior. Spanking is most appropriate for deliberate disobedience or defiance. (For thoughts on when and how spanking should be used as part of Reality Discipline, see the next subsection.) In this case, the parent wants to help her child "remember." My solution would be for Mom to tell her son that he gets one dry pair of underwear and pants a day. If he gets them wet, he comes into the house, takes off his soiled clothes, puts on his pajamas, and his day of play outside comes to an end. My guess is that having to spend one day, possibly two, indoors when he could be out playing should do a great deal for his memory.[3]

 "Forgetting" is both normal and convenient for preschoolers. What Reality Discipline can the small group devise for your forgetters?

Reality Discipline and Parents of "Middlers" (ages 6 to 12)

Talking Back

Like most parents, Jack has a real problem when his children "smart mouth" him. He wants his children to be able to say how they feel, but when Zelda crosses the line and becomes impudent, a little switch goes off in his brain: *You can't say that to me. Don't you know who I am? I'm your father!*

A Word About Spanking

Can "pulling the rug out" and letting children experience the consequences ever include spanking? Yes, I believe there are times a spanking is an appropriate response, but it rarely should be the first response. Here are some things to consider:

- Have you tried some other form of Reality Discipline? If the answer is yes, and the child is still willfully disobedient and defiant ("No, I won't!"), a spanking may be in order.

- Spanking is most appropriate for children in the two-to-seven age range. Children two years or younger should never be swatted. Conceptually, they don't understand what is happening. Also, spanking is totally inadvisable for children older than ten. Other consequences are more appropriate and more effective for adolescents and teenagers.

- Spanking should consist of two or three swats to the bottom, followed by holding the child and assuring him or her of your love.

- I personally believe you should use your hand rather than a neutral object, so that you are aware of how much pain is inflicted.

- Always take the child to a private place; never humiliate your child in public.

- Never spank when you are angry. A spanking should be a thoughtful action, not a hot-headed reaction to something that upsets you. A child should *never* be slapped, hit, punched, or kicked. Also, avoid spanking if you were abused as a child.

- No child is going to be harmed by an occasional spanking that follows the guidelines above. However, if you find you are spanking your children every day, back off and reevaluate the situation. Are your children getting lots of love, acceptance, and encouragement? Get professional counseling if needed.

Now, before some of you take out your ballpoint and let me know a thing or two about how spanking teaches violence to children, please consider the following. Did you know that those studies that "blast" spanking are based on kids who have been spanked at least twice a week? Sande and I have raised *five* children, and the total number of spankings given was a whopping eight! Rather a dramatic contrast from spanking each child 104 times a year. If all you're doing as a parent is spanking your children, then there is something wrong with your relationship. In fact, quite frankly, there is something wrong with you!

Talking back is another version of the power struggle. So the first rule is: Don't play the game! Eight-year-old Zelda is going to a birthday party but has gotten vocally abusive about the choices of clothing she's been given to wear. Jack has trouble keeping his temper, so he leaves the room for a minute or two. This conveys to the child, "I choose not to fight with you." But Jack is only gone a couple of minutes. He doesn't want Zelda to get the idea that she can "drive Daddy out" any time she wants. Once he has gotten control, he goes back and deals with the situation.

The first thing Jack does is send Zelda an "I" message. "I do not appreciate this kind of behavior and will not tolerate it." If Zelda continues to back-talk, she is the one who is removed from the scene and isolated for a brief time. Or Jack can "pull the rug out" by simply announcing, "I see you are choosing not to go to the party." (Don't use that as a threat and then withdraw. If you say it, mean it. Don't cave in when they whine and beg and say they are sorry. Follow through.)

On the other hand, if Zelda were three years younger and the back-talk was clearly defiant or abusive, a spanking might be in order. Jack makes sure he's in control of his emotions, and after the spanking he lets Zelda know how much he loves her, but he cannot let Zelda talk that way to her parents. (See subsection, "A Word About Spanking" on page 189.)

It is essential for women not to take any guff from their sons as well as for dads not to take any guff from their daughters. There is a very powerful relationship between a mother and her son and a dad and his daughter. What parents are really doing is training their children to learn who they are as male and female and what being a man or woman is all about. It is particularly important for mothers not to train their sons to believe that they can walk all over women.

Note-it

Never accept smart-mouth behavior. It is particularly important for mothers not to train sons to believe they can walk all over women. What parents are really doing is training their children what being a man or woman is all about.

> Do your children talk back occasionally, or every day? Brainstorm with the small group ways to bring Reality Discipline to bear.

Mealtimes

Remember, Reality Discipline offers a simple approach to dealing with the child who complains about the food or does not eat. You simply hold the child accountable for his or her choice. Remove the plate from the table, dump the food in the garbage, and excuse the child from the table. There are no further consequences—

but make it clear that the next time for eating is the next mealtime. (No between-meal snacks.) This works with ten-year-olds as well as three-year-olds.[4]

In single-parent homes, or when both parents have to work, assigning mealtime responsibilities to the children—peeling potatoes, making a salad, setting the table, taking out the garbage—is a beautiful opportunity to put the principles of Reality Discipline to work. "We're a family and everyone needs to pitch in to get dinner on."

But what if Mom and Dad come home and the table isn't set, the garbage hasn't been taken out, and dinner isn't started? Reality Discipline says to take action—but not the type of action you might think. Do not do any reminding, threatening, or blowing up. Simply sit down and read the paper. Wind down from your busy day. When the children come in and ask, "When's dinner going to be ready?" Mom or Dad can say matter-of-factly, "When the table has been set (potatoes peeled, garbage taken out, dishwasher loaded—whatever already has been assigned), dinner will be started."

This kind of response teaches children that order and cooperation are important to make a family function smoothly. Oh, yes, be sure you don't let your children "have dinner" by grabbing the nearest bag of chips and starting to munch away in front of the TV set. Let them know that no eating will be done until the responsibilities that were supposed to have been met are completed.

 What's mealtime like at your house? Share war stories and brainstorm Reality Discipline ideas with your small group.

Fighting and Sibling Rivalry

There is no way to eliminate rivalry between siblings. All you realistically can hope for is to minimize it. As you help your child learn to solve conflicts in a positive way, you build his psychological muscles for dealing with the realities of life.

Buddy and Betsy are six and eight. As the family is watching a TV program together, Buddy decides to pester his older sister by poking her. The first time he creates a disturbance, Dad takes him aside and says, "Buddy, you have a choice. You can sit quietly and watch the program with us or you can leave the room. You decide."

Dad and Buddy return to the family room, but Buddy persists in poking his sister. This time Dad uses action, not words. Buddy has made his "choice." Dad firmly but gently removes Buddy and puts him in his room for a stipulated amount of time—ten or fifteen minutes. At that time Dad tells him he may return when he is ready.

This approach calls for swift, decisive action, but at all times the parent is under control, not badgering, lecturing, bawling out, or swatting Buddy for his misbehavior. Dad is simply letting him learn through logical consequences that he cannot cause a ruckus when the family is trying to watch a television program.

Sometimes I have found that the best way to handle fighting is to give the children what they seem to want. If they want to fight, let them fight. Parents, however, have the right to say where the children can fight and under what conditions. If the children fight, it cannot interfere with the peace and welfare of others in the home. Guide them to a room elsewhere in the house, or possibly to the back yard. Give them instructions to continue fighting until they have worked out their problem. Leave them to their "fight." In most cases, when you give children permission to fight, they won't. They merely stand and look at each other. Children usually fight for attention. They want an audience. Take away the audience and the fight usually stops. The sooner parents learn to stay out of their children's hassles, the sooner they will teach their children greater responsibility and accountability. (Exception: do not use this strategy with children who are totally mismatched in size and strength.)

In every case, your goal is not to encourage fighting. You want your children to see that fighting is not a good way to solve problems. You want your children to learn that fighting gets no payoff from Mom and Dad, not even a negative one.

 Where and when do your children tend to fight? Brainstorm ways to bring a little Reality Discipline into their lives.

Getting Up

Whenever mothers or dads tell me it's a knock-down, drag-out battle to get little Buford out of bed and ready in time for school, I remind them of one of the basic principles of Reality Discipline: *you can't make another person do anything.* Let reality get your child up. After you have tried unsuccessfully a number of times to get your child up, simply remove yourself from all responsibility. Refuse to be used as a human alarm clock. Tell your child he will have to get himself up and off to school in the morning. Provide him with his own alarm clock. If he fails to get to school, the main reality will be big trouble with his teachers.

You may want to involve the child's teachers in your plan. Call the school and say that your child is going to be late because he has overslept and that you believe it would be a good idea if there were some definite consequences for his tardiness. When Buford arrives at school, his teacher might say, "Buford, I see you're late, but you're very lucky. You're going to be able to make up that twenty minutes you missed this morning by staying in at recess and doing some work while the rest of the kids go out and play."

Granted, calling Buford's bluff and letting him sleep in and be late for school is not an easy task or prospect. It can cause you anything from embarrassment to inconvenience—especially if you have to drive Buford to his school because the bus has already left by the time he's ready. (But don't drop everything so that he can still get there "on time." Do your own chores and take him when it's convenient for you.) If the school is anywhere within walking distance, however, let Buford be the one who's inconvenienced—let him walk.[5]

If you are a single parent or a working parent and do not have the flexibility to go into work late once or twice so you can allow Reality Discipline to take the above course with Buford, you might consider other alternatives. Depending on your place of employment, you might haul Buford to work with you until you have time at lunch to drop him at school. Or you might drop him at Aunt May's for the morning. Whatever you choose, make it as related to reality as possible without letting it be more fun than school.

 Can't get 'em up or move 'em out in the morning? Share your experiences and brainstorm some Reality Discipline that fits your situation.

Homework

Most teachers tell me that if a child "uses his minutes," he can get most of his homework done during free time while still at school. Of course, many children prefer to fritter away the minutes in other ways, and they have to take the assignments home. To help parents deal with homework hassles, I suggest several basic steps:

1. Provide an environment conducive to your child's way of learning. Some children need to sit at a desk or table with room to spread out their books and papers, free from distractions. Other children learn best curled up on the sofa with music playing to drown out distractions. People *do* have different learning styles. Get to know your child well enough to know what works best.

2. Invoke the rule: homework before TV. Never let a child do homework while watching TV. (They will try to convince you it can be done.) If a child's favorite show comes on during homework time, consider taping it for later viewing.

3. Don't do the child's homework for him! Parents, back off and refuse to get involved in homework to any great degree. If a child asks for help occasionally, that's another matter. But "occasionally" means exactly that.

If you don't watch it, you will soon be sucked into spending most of your evening hours with your child's schoolwork. It is much better for your child to earn a C than for you to help him or her get a B+ or an A.

4. Create logical consequences if homework is not completed. If at parent-teacher conference time you discover that your child didn't turn in five assignments, he might be grounded until he completes them. Or if at report card time his grades are not C or better, he might not be able to engage in extracurricular activities such as Little League. Talk with your child about what he thinks would be fair and work out something that sounds reasonable to both of you. The point is not to punish, but to create logical consequences so that schoolwork moves into its proper priority.

(Regarding grounding, parents usually ground kids only from things kids *want* to do. A better approach is to use short-term grounding—forty-eight hours maximum—where they go *nowhere*: not to youth group, not outside, not to Aunt Cindy's for dinner.)

 What are your homework hassles? Brainstorm ideas for Reality Discipline with your small group.

Irresponsibility

Paul, age ten, lived in a rural community and liked animals a great deal. Without his parents' permission, he bought (with his own money) two baby pigs from another boy. But Mom wasn't ready for baby pigs and told him he would have to get rid of the little porkers. Two weeks later, however, the pigs were still there. Paul had used all the tricks on his parents: the other boy had already spent Paul's money, so he couldn't take them back; he would take good care of them; he'd sell them and even make some money, and so on.

The whole thing was turning into something of a family pork-barrel scandal when the parents sought me out as counsel. My recommendation was swift and brief: get rid of the pigs. Their response beautifully illustrates the dilemma parents find themselves in when they're not willing to pull the rug out. "How can we get rid of the pigs when they belong to Paul? And where could we take them?" I pointed out that their child had been irresponsible when he brought home two animals without the consent of his parents. As Paul's parents, they were in authority over him—something parents easily forget these days. When a child's actions say, "You're not my authority—I'll do my own thing," parents have the responsibility to act quickly and decisively—and pull the rug out.

Paul's parents got the message. They got rid of the pigs rather easily by finding another family who was willing to take them—without having to pay for them. Of course, when Paul discovered his pigs were gone, he was outraged. He lost all the money it cost him to buy the two pigs. But Mom and Dad had been very patient during the two weeks they had reminded him to get rid of the pigs. There was a good possibility he could have taken them back to the farm where he had bought them and gotten his money back. But Paul was so determined to do his own thing that he didn't even bother to try.

As I'm sure you have already suspected, the pig incident wasn't an isolated case in Paul's life. He had already been "doing his own thing" in many different ways. But his parents told me later that this "rug-pulling incident" with the pigs really got Paul's attention and led to some positive changes in his behavior.[6]

 Do your children sometimes act irresponsibly, leaving you holding the bag? Brainstorm ways to put responsibility back on your child's shoulders.

Reality Discipline for Parents of Teenagers

My son, Kevin, was about fifteen years old when he engaged me in a lively discussion regarding the new "pump-them-up" athletic shoes. He was so psyched up about them that I knew the pitch was coming. Finally he got to it: "Dad, can I get them? They cost a hundred dollars."

"Sure," I calmly said. "Sounds like interesting shoes."

"When can I get them?"

"As soon as you get the hundred dollars! In fact, if you can earn two hundred, you can get two pair."

Now, I wasn't trying to be insensitive to his heart's desire, but we need to learn to give our children what they need, not what they want. As a parent who can afford to give my children anything they want, I take great pride in *not* giving them "Jack diddly squat!" We give them love, time, and prayer. But we really go easy on material things!

Much of our approach to the situations arising with teenagers as well as younger children could be informed by the principle, "Give them what they need, not what they want."

Clean Room

What parent doesn't despair over that teenage fiasco, The Messy Room! But even though it's hard to do, parents need to quit nagging and haranguing and let reality take over. One approach to the messy room is simply to tell your teenager, "Since you don't want to keep your room even moderately clean, please keep the door closed. Of course, I won't be able to find any of your dirty clothes in the mess, so you will have to do your own laundry from here on out." Now that's reality!

Another option is the Responsibilities/Privileges Approach. If your sixteen-year-old wants a filthy room, he can have it, but he foregoes the car keys, assuming he has a license and is using your car. Let your son know that fulfilling his responsibilities at home is his first priority. If he can't be responsible at home, he's not ready for the responsibilities of operating a car on public highways.

Still another option is to say, "Let's make a deal. During the week, you keep your door shut. On Saturday, however, we expect you to shovel out your room and put it in generally good order before going out with your friends." Then give your teenager every opportunity to meet that responsibility.

 Tired of pulling out your hair over The Messy Room? Brainstorm ideas for Reality Discipline with other bald members of your small group.

Parties

If we could come up with an absolutely foolproof answer to the problem of parties, we might bottle and sell it and make enough to put a good dent in the national debt! But here are some options to try with your teenager:

Don't necessarily take your teenager's word about the "facts" of a party. Not that your teen is intentionally lying. But where a party is concerned, your teenager hears about it from a friend who is "sure" that so-and-so's mother will be home to supervise, and so on. Sometimes the actual facts of the situation get lost in the enthusiasm.

One mother I know makes it a policy always to call the home where the party will be held. She talks directly to the parent who will be supervising, and asks what videos will be shown and what they intend to do if any alcohol or uninvited guests show up. If she hears something that makes her uneasy (for example, the video is R-rated), she asks the host or hostess politely if another choice could be made, as her daughter is not allowed to watch R-rated movies. More often than not, this mother said, the parent is surprised that another parent is concerned enough to call. (One time this particular mother discovered that the "supervising" parent had agreed to go next door while the party was in progress. My friend said that wasn't acceptable and her daughter would not be able to come. To her surprise, the other mother agreed to be present in the home during the party after all.)

Another father, whose fourteen-year-old son drank beer at supposedly supervised parties, said, "I

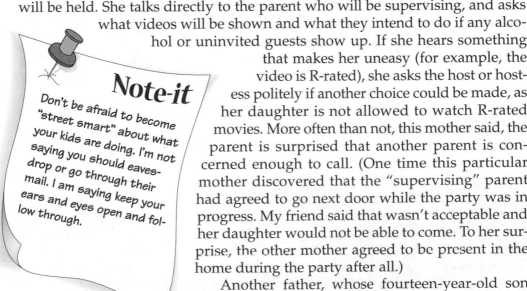

Note-it

Don't be afraid to become "street smart" about what your kids are doing. I'm not saying you should eavesdrop or go through their mail. I am saying keep your ears and eyes open and follow through.

tried to tell our son that it's illegal and we don't approve," but the son just shrugged and said he liked the "buzz" he got from drinking beer. These parents needed to exercise some "tough love." They needed to state unequivocally that teenage drinking is illegal and that they would not tolerate it. If the son continued to drink beer, even at supervised parties, he would forego certain privileges that he loved dearly—no help with getting his driver's license or permission to drive the family car comes to mind. If this teenager was that into drinking alcohol because he "likes the buzz," he certainly wasn't ready to be granted the responsibility and privilege of driving a car.

Don't be afraid to become "street smart" about what your kids are doing. I'm not saying that you should eavesdrop when they're on the phone, go through their mail, or anything like that. I am saying keep your ears and eyes open for offhand remarks, and follow through by contacting other parents to see if they know where and when a party might be taking place. Then band together and talk to the parents who will be supervising the party. Tell them, in no uncertain terms, that you do not want alcohol served and, if it is served, your son or daughter simply can't attend. Don't be afraid of offending them. Your kids' lives are at stake!

And don't forget: Making your home "kid-friendly" and allowing your teenager to have a party at your house occasionally are the best options of all. Sit down with your teen and agree on what activities are appropriate, what the rules are, and how cleanup is going to happen. Sure, it blows an evening, but it may be an investment worth making.

 Party time! And it's giving you gray hair. Don't panic—brainstorm some Reality Discipline ideas with your fellow parents-of-teens.

Dating

Your fourteen-year-old daughter is very mature and physically developed for her age. She wants to date a boy who is three years older. She has never officially dated before and you think she's too young. How can you best handle this?

Sit down with your daughter and say something like this: "Honey, you may not want to hear this, but your mother and I agree that you can't go on single dates at fourteen, particularly with a boy who is three years older. We think that sixteen is a much more realistic age to start single dating."

Your daughter will probably protest that you don't trust her, she's not that kind of girl, he's not that kind of boy, and so on. Tell her, "Honey, we believe you and we trust you. We also have the responsibility not to let you get into situations that put you at risk."

Don't be afraid to take a stand and do all you can to discourage this budding relationship between your daughter and someone three years older. When "John" discovers that he can't get your daughter out alone in his car, that may be enough

Note-it

Before age sixteen, group dates and get-togethers might be okay, but even a double date doesn't guarantee proper behavior. In fact, the other couple may simply serve as a role model for how to get into trouble.

to end the relationship. He may suddenly find it convenient to be interested in someone else. On the other hand, John may not go away that easily. Then you must control the situation as best you can. Don't hesitate to set up strict rules about what is allowed and not allowed. For one thing, do not let your daughter accept rides home from school in John's car, which can quickly turn into a "date" that could escalate into the very activities you fear. If John wants to see your daughter, he can come over to the house to spend time watching television, studying, and the like, but only when at least one parent is home. You should also talk to John's parents and share your specific concerns.

Above all, while being firm, be loving and gentle. Keep in mind that many teenagers want to be parented. For all you know, your daughter may be somewhat fearful of dating John, but she is having trouble bucking her peer group, who thinks she is crazy for turning down a seventeen-year-old stud with a nice car.

I encourage parents to make a clear rule: No single dating until age sixteen. Group dates and get-togethers might be okay, but even beware of "double dates." A double date hardly guarantees proper behavior. In fact, the other couple may simply serve as a role model for how to get into a situation your daughter isn't ready for at all.[7]

 Does your teen want to start dating? Share experiences with the other parents in your small group and brainstorm some Reality Discipline.

Curfew

Curfew falls into the category of privileges. If your fourteen-year-old handles his 10:30 weekend curfew in a responsible way, you can add on a half hour at age fifteen and so forth throughout high school. Don't be afraid to set curfews and stick to them. As one street-wise youth worker says wryly, "Nothing good happens after midnight." It's always better to start with an earlier time and make exceptions in special situations than to start with midnight and have nowhere to go.

We let our children know we are flexible if a special situation comes up—but we ask them to call us and check in. If you go to bed before they come in (you probably won't sleep!), ask your teens to knock on your bedroom door when they get in. If curfew is ignored, however, reality sets in. Lecturing and yelling are useless, not to mention ineffective. If a sixteen-year-old with a new driver's license is irresponsible about his 11:30 curfew, then some Reality Discipline options are

(a) come in half an hour earlier next time, (b) not go out with friends the next week-end, or (c) give up the car keys. As your teen hits seventeen or eighteen, and if he or she has been basically responsible about curfew so far, you might give him or her more responsibility for deciding on a reasonable curfew.

 So, lost many nights of sleep recently? Ask what other parents have done about curfew and apply the principles of Reality Discipline.

Nagging

In many homes Mom and Dad constantly remind their children to do things they are expected to do. One teenage girl, tired of being nagged all the time, shocked her mother by saying, "Why should I try to remember anything? You do all my remembering for me." This mother was teaching her daughter to be irresponsible by reminding her when to leave for school, not to forget her job interview, to clean her room, and so on.

Reality Discipline has an answer for the problem: *Stop doing all that reminding!* Let your children know that you are going to tell them things only once. Then let Reality Discipline take over. If you tell your daughter that her room needs to be clean (responsibility) before she can go out with friends (privilege), commit yourself to carry through. If the room is not clean when the friends arrive to pick her up, she doesn't go. Don't feel guilty; it's your teenager's choice. (My friend's mistake: she wanted her daughter to be able to go out, and also wanted to avoid a scene, so she reminded her daughter throughout the day about the room to help her avoid the consequence!)

My advice is: Only set up consequences you're ready and willing to follow through on! My friend finally got the message. She started assigning consequences that she was only too happy to impose—like doing dishes or losing TV or phone privileges—as an added incentive not to nag her daughter. After all, she might get the TV or phone to herself for a change!

 Are you nagging your teenager all the time? Ask the small group to help you come up with some Reality Discipline instead!

Telephone

Evie picked up the extension phone in her room four or five times in less than five minutes while Mom was on the kitchen phone talking to a friend. Mom had clearly spelled out to her daughter that she was not to interrupt while other people were on the phone. It would have been no hardship for Evie to come out to the kitchen to see when Mom had hung up, then go back into her own room and use the special extension that Dad had installed just for her a few months ago.

After Mom hung up, she went to the teenager's room and, without lectures or yelling, simply told her she was taking Evie's extension and putting it away for a week.

"A week?" Evie cried, aghast. "What for?"

"For not living up to our agreement," Mom said calmly. "You know you aren't supposed to interrupt while others are on the phone. So you will have to do without your own extension for a week. You may still make calls from the kitchen phone."

Got teenagers all over your phone? Share phone stories with the small group and brainstorm some Reality Discipline for different situations.

At the end of your time together, come back together in the whole group. Conclude with the following comments and then pray for one another as you put Reality Discipline into practice this week.

In summary, never forget that children expect adults to discipline them. If the discipline is loving, it will be geared toward instruction, teaching, guiding, and above all, holding a child accountable for his or her actions. When a parent doesn't discipline a child, that parent invites rebellion. Children can actually develop hatred toward their parents if the parents don't take a stand and discipline them.

When our oldest child, Holly, was seven years old, she gave me the following note for Father's Day. The original hangs on my office wall:

> World's Gatist Father,
> My father is the gratist,
> Your the best, caring, loveing
> THE BEST ! ! ! ! !
> Even when you disaplin me,
> I love you the same,
> Love, Holly

Naturally I like the "World's Gatist Father" line, but I am more impressed that Holly used the term *discipline* rather than the word *punish*. Children *want* us to discipline them because the act of discipline shows we care.[8]

Portions of this session were adapted from:

Leman, Dr. Kevin. *Bringing Up Kids Without Tearing Them Down* (chapters 9 through 11). Nashville, Tenn.: Nelson, 1995.

Leman, Dr. Kevin. *Making Children Mind Without Losing Yours* (chapter 7). Grand Rapids, Mich.: Revell, 1984.

For further information, consider:

Campbell, Ross. *How to Really Love Your Teenager.* Wheaton, Ill.: Victor, 1981.

NOTES

1. Adapted from Dr. Kevin Leman, *Making Children Mind Without Losing Yours.* (Grand Rapids, Mich.: Fleming H. Revell, a division of Baker Book House Company, 1984), pp. 133–135.
2. The preceding paragraphs were adapted from Dr. Kevin Leman, *Bringing Up Kids Without Tearing Them Down* (chapters 9 through 11). Nashville, Tenn.: Thomas Nelson Publishers, 1995, p. 241.
3. Adapted from *Bringing Up Kids . . .*, pp. 245-246.
4. Adapted from *Bringing Up Kids . . .*, p. 160.
5. Adapted from *Making Children Mind . . .*, pp. 149-150.
6. Adapted from *Making Children Mind . . .*, pp. 67-69.
7. Adapted from *Bringing Up Kids . . .*, pp. 323-324.
8. Adapted from *Making Children Mind . . .*, pp. 30-31.

Are We Having Fun Yet?
Putting Relationships First

The unqualified love that Almighty God gives to us is the same kind of unconditional love that we need to give to our children. But do they want in on it?
You bet! I think kids clearly tell us they want in on this love. If you have any
doubts, try this little experiment if you have children between the ages of two-and-
a-half and five. (I affectionately refer to them as the "ankle-biter battalion.")

With your husband or wife, go into the kitchen and embrace each other, hug,
and kiss. Within 4.6 seconds—I don't know how they know this—but the little
ankle-biters will come like torpedoes out of left and right field and they will wiggle
in right between you. Why? Because children are the
enemy? No, no. Because they want to be a part of that
loving union. Children want to belong.

Sometimes in the "daily battle" of parenting—when
you're juggling job, laundry, runny noses, peanut butter on
the light switch, lost homework, temper tantrums, sibling
fights, and teenage sulks—it's easy to lose sight of the bottom line that makes family life hang together. Paraphras-
ing a popular political slogan: "It's the relationship, stupid!"

As I mentioned in session 10, Josh McDowell, popular
speaker on college and high school campuses, has a favorite
saying: "Rules without relationships lead to rebellion." I
revised what he said to create my last principle of Reality
Discipline: "You put relationships before rules." Of course you
love your kids—but do you have a *relationship* with them?

When I say this in a seminar, some parents interpret this to mean we should try
to make our children happy all of the time. I pull them up short when I say, "Not at
all. One of the things I want to make sure I do is help you produce unhappy children—at least some of the time. Of course, I hope they'll be happy and content most

of the time, but sometimes it is appropriate for your children to be unhappy. We call it 'Reality Discipline' for a reason."

What I mean by saying that "you put relationships before rules" is that training and discipline are most effective in a context of love, respect, and enjoying one another in the family. The total package (love *and* limits) translates to something more enduring than mere fun and happiness. How about peace, order, and joy?

More than a Few Laughs

The goal of happiness or having fun is far too shallow for God's purposes in our families. As we have seen throughout these sessions, our task is to bring up our children "in the training and instruction of the Lord" (Ephesians 6:4).

 Look up the following references in the book of Proverbs and record how our "training in the Lord" affects the whole family. Find the answer key at the end of the session on page 217.

Proverbs 2:1-5; 3:1-2; 5:23; 6:20-23; 15:10; 17:21b,25; 19:18; 22:15; 23:15,16,24; 29:15,17.

Results of "training in the Lord" For parents:	Results of no "training in the Lord" For parents:
1.	1.
2.	2.
3.	3.
4.	4.

For children:	For children:
1.	1.
2.	2.
3.	3.
4.	
5.	
6.	
7.	

How do we create this home where "training in the Lord" can take place? What kinds of relationships are necessary for "discipline" and "training" to have the most positive effect? The context for Reality Discipline is relationships built on respect, trust, enjoying our children, keeping things in perspective, and even grace and forgiveness.

Respect Is a Two-Way Street

Authoritarian parents often make their children "toe the mark" by demanding respect, and woe unto the kid who doesn't give it to them. What these parents don't realize is that they are not getting respect, they are only receiving their children's begrudging obedience, which comes out of fear. The children are biding their time, and there will come a day for payback. I deal frequently with families where the "respectful" child has decided to pay back the parents in dramatic and even devastating ways.

On the other hand, being respectful of your kids doesn't mean you put them in charge. After all, you are the adults and you are in healthy authority over your kids. Never forget that. You can still be firm in stating your expectations, but at the same time remember that all the expectations in the world will not do you much good if you act disrespectfully toward your children and treat them like second-class citizens, or worse.

I often suggest to parents that they check themselves on how they are talking to their children as they try to do everyday correcting and teaching. What does your child hear? Are your comments harsh and disrespectful or firm but respectful? There's a difference you probably wouldn't have too much trouble discerning if someone else were speaking to you in that manner.[1]

Note-it

Don't take misbehavior personally. Every child is going to misbehave at one time or another in life. Your job is to roll with it, to take it in stride, and yet remain in healthy authority.

Don't Discipline in Public

Suppose your child has said or done something discourteous to another person — child or adult. As I have been known to say, "Move right in and take the little buzzard by the beak." In other words, it's best to deal with the behavior then and there.

But do not reprimand your child in front of the offended party. Try to remove your child from the room, or at least go off a short distance, and then speak to him. Gently but firmly tell your child exactly what your feelings are about what he just said or did and why you feel that way. If the child is old enough (about three years or above), have him go back to the offended party and apologize. If the child refuses to do so, you may want to go to another form of discipline such as isolation: remove him from the group for a set period of time.

What you should always seek, if at all possible, is to have the child say, "I'm sorry, please forgive me," or "Excuse me"—something that will convey to the offended person that the child is sorry.

I repeat, the best way to teach this kind of courtesy is to practice it yourself. If you ever offend your child or your spouse, be willing to say, "I'm sorry," without hesitation.[2]

Provide Choices

The source of many power struggles between parent and child is the child's bid for respect. Mother says Betsy will wear a certain dress and Betsy says she won't. Mother says she will and Betsy firmly resists again. And the war is on.

How can this kind of struggle be avoided? How can Mom teach her daughter to respect parental wishes? The obvious answer is for Mom to try to show her daughter some respect as well. And how can Mom accomplish this without giving up all of her authority? One possibility is to separate the clothes in Betsy's closet: put clothes for play and school on one side and clothes for Sunday school, church, and special occasions on the other. Then Betsy can make a choice and feel that she has some control over her own life.

Through this simple arrangement, you will allow your child to make more and more decisions for herself, which builds self-esteem and confidence. The child feels respected and in turn will be more likely to respect the parent. I have found it interesting that when a parent gives a certain amount of freedom to a child regarding choice of what the child might wear, the child often comes out dressed and asks for Mom's or Dad's approval concerning what he or she has on. This is just one simple example of a basic principle: if we do our job as parents and use our authority wisely, our children will respect us and our opinions.[3]

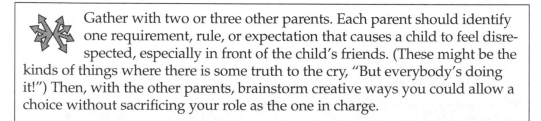 Gather with two or three other parents. Each parent should identify one requirement, rule, or expectation that causes a child to feel disrespected, especially in front of the child's friends. (These might be the kinds of things where there is some truth to the cry, "But everybody's doing it!") Then, with the other parents, brainstorm creative ways you could allow a choice without sacrificing your role as the one in charge.

Extend Your Trust When Possible

How often have you heard an adult say, "If you don't want to be treated like a baby, start acting your age"? That *might* pass as Reality Discipline under unique circumstances, but all too often it represents nothing more than a parent's angry retort.

It's true that children often don't act their age, slipping back into younger behaviors out of self-indulgence or to manipulate you. However, sometimes we parents don't "catch them being good" so we can acknowledge they're maturing. Time goes by much faster than we realize, and we are still keeping twelve-year-old Roger on the same leash we used when he was ten. Or we haven't extended seventeen-year-old Sally's curfew even though she has proved responsible for over a year.

During her junior year in high school, our daughter Krissy went to an out-of-town football game. At 11:30 that night she called me from a pizza parlor and wanted to know what time she had to get home. I replied, "Honey, you know what time to be home."

"No, I don't," she responded. "What time do I have to be home?"

"Just be home at a reasonable time," was all I said.

"But, Dad, we won the game, but the team hasn't gotten here yet."

At this point I was getting the picture. The game was over and Krissy and her other friends were waiting for the team to come by the pizza parlor to celebrate their victory.

"So, you want to wait for the team—that's why you're there, and that's why you're calling."

"Well, yeah, exactly," Krissy said hesitantly.

"Well, Honey, I appreciate your calling. Go ahead and wait for the team, enjoy yourself, and be home at a reasonable hour."

Forty-five minutes later Krissy called back a second time to remind me what time it was, and I again reminded her to be home at a reasonable time. She finally got home at 12:50 A.M.

Now, all this may sound as if I was a permissive dad, but I don't think so. At the time, Krissy was seventeen years old. She had already been driving for over a year and had proved herself very responsible. She called me twice during the evening to be sure that I knew where she was and what was happening. Normally, 12:50 A.M. is a bit late to be getting in, but under the circumstances, I think it was acceptable. And in extending my trust, I showed a great deal of respect for her.[4]

Honor Their Privacy

By the time children become teens, do your best to provide private rooms to which they can retreat, pursue their hobbies, listen to their music, and store their junk. Don't read their letters or listen in on their phone calls.

This should be your general policy unless you are dealing with dangerous or illegal behavior. And then, don't be a fool or stick your head in the sand!

The question of moral standards concerning entertainment should be settled apart from the question of privacy. Of course, there are kinds of music or videos or other forms of entertainment that are not welcome in your house, and a private room is not an excuse to violate those standards. On the other hand, no parent should expect to *enjoy* listening to all of his or her teenager's music, even if it is within acceptable bounds. So give them a place to enjoy it.

Don't Demand Respect

If you are the parent of a teenager, you probably know the feeling of driving your kids to school and having them sink into the car seat as you get closer and closer to the school. And of course you're driving the ugly four-door with black sidewalls. Why couldn't you buy a Camaro or something nice for your teenager? Anyway, your teenager says to you, "Uh, Mom, just drop me off at the corner."

Note-it

If communication with your children has not been good, don't assume they'll open up the minute you say you're ready to listen. It'll take time before they believe that your interest is more than a passing fad.

"But Honey, we're three-quarters of a mile from school."

"Well, I've got these new shoes, and I thought I'd just break them in by walking."

But being embarrassed to be identified with us in public is not nearly so disrespectful as the behavior that says, "Stay away from me." "Get off my case." "Get out of my life." "Give me space." "Lighten up, chill out, and back off!" "Don't have a cow, man."

It's tempting to get in their face and say, "Do you know who you're talking to? I'm your father!" Demanding respect may achieve the appearance of compliance at the moment—if you're bigger than they are—but you haven't really won anything. Instead, you might indeed back off and wait for what educators call "a teachable moment" when the importance of mutual respect can be demonstrated in a humorous but effective way.

For instance, yesterday your teenager told you to "get out of my life." Today he walks in and says, "Hey, Dad, can I take the car tonight?" You finally respond—after pretending you don't hear him until he asks three times—"Who, me? Oh, well, I'd love to help you son, but right now I'm outta your life."

In your same groups of four or five people identify the three most common areas where you feel a lack of respect from your children. Then identify the three areas where your children may question your respect for them. Finally, by yourself, write out a commitment for one way you can reinforce your respect for your children. (Note: You may want to do this activity for each of your children.)

How we feel our children disrespect us:

1.

2.

3.

How we disrespect our children:

1.

2.

3.

I commit myself to show greater respect for my children this next week by . . . (provide a separate commitment for each child):

Lighten Up and Enjoy Your Children

When it comes to the process of training your children in the Lord, which saying is most likely to describe your approach?

- ■ "Rome was not built in a day" (an old English proverb recorded in 1546 by John Heywood).[5]

- ■ Or "Rome, if built at all, must be built in a day" (attributed to Marcus Cato who died in 149 B.C.).[6]

Many parents act like today is all the time they've got—or are willing to invest—in raising their children. From birth until age eighteen, they are on a frantic track to pack in everything they can. But that destroys the joy of family and hurts you and your children.

Free the Hurried Child

Dr. David Elkind did us all a favor by writing the book, *The Hurried Child*, in which he pointed out the terrible price our children pay when we force them to grow up so fast. I also love the title of his sequel: *All Grown Up and No Place to Go*. It's really crazy what we're doing to kids today. We hurry our little tykes off to preschool, off to kiddie college; we want to get them in the *right* kiddie college. We have graduations for four-year-olds. I mean, it's a little crazy. We need to return children to the place of just being a child.

I don't know how many of you have ever gone to a T-ball game where the little kids hit the ball on a stick. Hey, it's a kick and a half; it really is. One day I was out for a walk and stumbled upon one of these games, and I thought, *Hey, this looks good,* being a baseball player from way back. So I stood there next to the cage and watched for only a few minutes—what I saw was unbelievable. I'll never forget it. A ground ball got hit out to center field. Now, a ground ball in that league could be a grand slam. And the ball's going over second base, out toward the center fielder, and I notice something's a little weird. The center fielder was on all fours.

Apparently, the parents were directly behind me in the cheering section, and they start yelling and screaming, "Michael, Michael, get the ball! It's right there, Michael. Get the ball!"

But Michael was still on all fours. Finally, he looks up, cups his hands to his mouth, and yells, "I'm looking for a four-leaf clover."

I thought, *Something is amiss here.*

In a few minutes the inning was over, and the kids came running in. But they headed right for the coach, begging, "Can we sit? Can we sit now?"

The coach, thinking they were asking if they could "hit," said, "Hey, you know the rules, look on the tree over there, line up according to your batting order."

But they didn't want to hit. The game had barely started—the top of the first inning—and they already wanted to sit. I started thinking, *Why are these kids playing T-ball?*

It's no wonder that for years now, seven- and eight-year-old kids have been showing up in my office stressed out. I ask you, why should a seven- or eight-year-old kid be stressed out in life? This ought to be a time of fun, of learning about themselves and about others. If they want to learn one activity or sport, fine, but take it easy. Rome was *not* built in a day!

List your children's out-of-the-home activities; include school, church— everything. Being as ruthless as you can, evaluate each activity according to how essential it is for your child right now, how much the activity is *your* idea, and how much your child values the activity. Score each category 1 through 5, with 5 being high. Use a separate sheet of paper if necessary. Then ask yourself, "What's driving my children?"

Child's Name: _____

Activities	Necessity	My Idea	His/Her Idea
1.			
2.			
3.			
4.			
5.			

Child's Name: _____

Activities	Necessity	My Idea	His/Her Idea
1.			
2.			
3.			
4.			
5.			

Child's Name: _____

Activities	Necessity	My Idea	His/Her Idea
1.			
2.			
3.			
4.			
5.			

The Harried Parent

Take this advice and you won't feel so much like the woman for whom I named a chapter in one of my books: "Help, I'm a Cabbie, and My Minivan Isn't Even Yellow." Think about it: What would life be like without your kids being in all those activities? Maybe you'd find more family time. After all, bonding with the family is really what is going to imprint on your children's lives and give them the ability to face their peer group in as healthy a way as possible.

When does all this pressure start? At a very early age. For instance, I'll pick on you, Mom. You're at a coffee with some girlfriends from church. Like most moms, before too long the conversation drifts to your precious children. Potty training comes up, and one mother mentions that her Brittany, who is only twenty-one months, is already toilet trained. Then she turns to you and asks, "How old is Melissa now?"

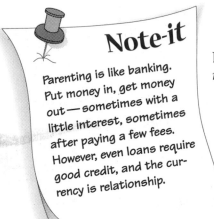

Note-it

Parenting is like banking. Put money in, get money out — sometimes with a little interest, sometimes after paying a few fees. However, even loans require good credit, and the currency is relationship.

"Oh, she's twenty-six months."

"And how long has she been toilet trained?"

You stammer, "Well, we're still working on it." But inside you're telling yourself, *Oh, my goodness, my child is falling behind!*

All of us want our kids to succeed, so it's real easy to get into this trap of pushing kids ahead too early in life. Parents, slow down! Grant your children their childhood. Remember, they're small for such a short period of time, so take the time with them to enjoy every step as they grow through these wonderful years.

Try a Family Night

I'm afraid many parents push their children onto a hectic treadmill of out-of-the-home, organized activities because they don't know what to do with their children when they are home together.

Singing around the piano doesn't seem to measure up to MTV, and fishing with Dad lacks the glamour of flag football with helmets and uniforms and big shiny trophies. Table games and popcorn pale compared to a movie at the mall. And whoever heard of spending all winter building a sailboat in the garage when you could buy a fiberglass one in an afternoon? There may be nothing wrong with some of these shortcuts or higher powered activities, but to what degree have we sacrificed time together to enjoy them?

If you have trouble thinking of ideas to do with your children, look up one of the many books that offer ideas for "priming your pump."

 From the samples listed below, select one activity that your family can try this next week.

___ A breakfast grace to sing together around the table

___ Dressing up for a family supper, either formally or in costumes

___ Boycott TV and all evening meetings (even church meetings) for one week to read a whole novel aloud together

___ An all-family Saturday "work morning" with work-together activities, followed by going bowling

___ A traditional Jewish Sabbath meal

___ A family "meeting" to make some major decision or resolve some problems

___ A weekend retreat for just one parent and one child

___ Hosting a "tea" for guests

___ Creating family photo albums or going through some old ones

___ Visiting an old-folks home
___ A family bike ride in the forest preserve
___ A nonbirthday party, drawing names and giving crazy $1 gifts to each other
___ Other ideas:

 This next section will be more interesting and useful if you review different ways to approach content sections on page 16 of the introduction.

Relationships Come Before Rules

When children are young, they are usually eager to please you, crawl on your lap, give you a hug. And then something happens. Around age eleven or twelve or thirteen, if Mom says it or suggests it or wears it, it's definitely not cool. Your teen acts as if he would rather die than be seen at the mall with his parents. You say cheerfully, "Hi! How was your day?" and hostility bristles as though you'd invaded enemy airspace.

But don't be fooled. Even adolescents—the kids in the hormone group—want to belong. My daughter, Krissy, comes to mind again. Her first high school volleyball game as a new member of the team was an away game. At dinner before the game she announced that *no one* from the family was to go to the game. *No one!* But, being the father of the family and realizing that authority has its God-given privileges, I responded with a Cheshire-cat grin and a wiggle of my eyebrows, "Krissy, I'm going to be there."

"No, Dad. No! You're not going to be there. Don't come!" she pleaded. "If you come, Dad, please don't you yell."

She was so excited, so nervous about her game. It was funny. The game was ninety miles from our home. It was not a quick trip, but I got in the car and drove those ninety miles, arriving only a few minutes late. The game had already begun when I slipped into an end seat on the bleachers.

There was Krissy Leman, out there in her set position with her little hands on those knees at age fifteen. I was a good seventy-five feet away, way over in the corner, but she saw me. And I was rewarded by the fingers on her left hand going up and down a couple times, just to acknowledge, "Dad, I see you're here."

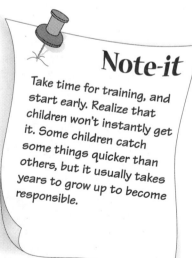

Note-it
Take time for training, and start early. Realize that children won't instantly get it. Some children catch some things quicker than others, but it usually takes years to grow up to become responsible.

Never Put the Relationship on the Line

When some friends of mine had a major confrontation with their teenage daughter over a boyfriend—of whom they did not approve—things came right down to the wire. Would she obey? Or would they have to take drastic measures to break it up?

When the older brother came home from college and saw how tense the family was, he became alarmed. On the one hand, he agreed that the boyfriend (five years older and living on his own) was not healthy for his sister. The boyfriend manipulated her and drew her into situations inappropriate for her age even though he was very immature and emotionally dependent on her. On the other hand, the brother sensed that his sister was on the verge of doing something foolish to exert her independence.

Privately, the older brother talked to his parents. "Whatever you do, don't put your relationship with Sis on the line. She's going to need you for a long time to come, but you won't have any influence if you lose her while trying to save her from this guy."

To his sister he pleaded in much the same way. "You're going to need a relationship with the folks for a long time to come no matter what you do. Don't forfeit that by some angry act now."

Fortunately, my friends listened to their son and looked harder for some kind of a compromise. They decided that if they had to deal with this joker, it was better that his feet be under their dining room table than having their daughter sneak off to his apartment. So they said to their daughter, "We're not going to prohibit you from seeing him, but it's gotta start happening here, at our house, unless you're on a formal date in a public place." At first, she was suspicious, but underneath it all, their concession represented something she secretly wanted, for Mom and Dad to accept her choice in a friend.

Once the daughter no longer had to fight her parents for a sense of autonomy, it did not take long—about four months—for her to see the jerk for who he was and break up with him on her own.

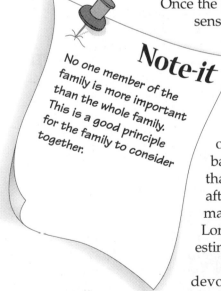

Note-it

No one member of the family is more important than the whole family. This is a good principle for the family to consider together.

Teach Relationally

Hannah, my eleven-year-old daughter, was part of a musical at her school, and the music was all based upon Scripture. One song highlighted the fact that God is our strength and shield. The morning after the musical, I told her that I was wondering how many kids really knew what it meant to have the Lord be their strength and shield. We had a very interesting conversation on the way to school.

Now this, by the way, is what I consider family devotions: Looking for openings in a child's life to share the truth that God's Word is practical and relevant for everyday living.

So I asked Hannah if she knew what having God as our source of strength really meant. And she said, "Well, I think so."

I said, "Let me ask you a question. If you did something bad in school, something that you didn't want Mommy and Daddy to know about, what should you do?"

She said, "Well, pray about it."

I said, "Good. You'd pray to God, and you'd ask Him for guidance about what to do concerning this problem. And after you'd prayed to God and asked for His guidance, what kind of answer do you think you'd get back for that prayer?"

She paused for a moment and then she said, "Well, to tell you and Mom."

I said, "Right. And how would you feel after you'd told me and Mom?"

"Better," she said.

"But what would happen if you didn't tell Mommy and Daddy. Remember, you tried to hide it from us earlier. So how would you feel?"

"Bad."

I said, "See? There's an example of going to God for your strength, the strength to tell us. He is your strength. He is your source of power. What about the shield part?"

She said, "Oh, I know that, Daddy. You know, in the book of Ephesians it talks about putting on the armor of God."

I said, "You are very right. And that's why if we read God's Word and watch and listen for opportunities in our life to put that Scripture to the test, every day we get a confirmation that God, through His Holy Spirit, is living in us and guiding our life."

Another example that comes to mind involved my six-year-old Lauren. One morning as I said good-bye to her at her kindergarten, I reminded her that Daddy had to fly on the airplane. Usually when I tell her this, she groans and says things like, "Oh, Daddy, I don't want you to go on the airplane." I then assure her that I'll be back in one or two days or whenever. But I always assure her that I'll be praying for her. And then I ask her to pray for me, and she does!

Family devotions aren't necessarily huddling around the fireplace or reading the Bible at the dinner table. Family devotions are simply the many ways we show each other devotion to God and to each other.

These are the kinds of opportunities I cherish as a dad, little openings that, if I'll just have an open mind and spirit, I can use to share the reality of God's love for each of us and His plan for us.

Grace, Forgiveness, and Redemption

One theological definition of *grace* is "unmerited favor." When we didn't deserve to be let off, God nevertheless forgave us. Sometimes as a parent you can redeem your relationship with your child by granting grace. Care must be taken to be sure that your response is not lazy permissiveness or irresponsible inconsistency, but occasionally you can shock a child out of a power struggle or a bad pattern by doing the totally unexpected.

For instance, if mealtime has become a war zone, here's a strategy you might try: Commit yourself to breaking the typical mealtime routine. Do not nag or coax your children to eat their vegetables or to finish their milk. Do not remind your children to clean their plates. Don't waste your breath with stories about people in Africa who are starving to death. Your children know there is no way to send them any of the food the family has been served for that meal anyway.

Note-it

The more transparent we are as parents, the more authentic we are, and the more approachable we become. If you want kids to talk, to communicate with you and tell you what's really going on, put yourself in that position.

Instead, have everyone sit down to dinner, but don't bother to put food on the plates of your children. Let the children ask for things to be passed. Let them take exactly what they want. Basically ignore what they are eating or not eating. Then sit back and listen. See if the conversation around the table changes. Talk about subjects of interest to you and to your children. Do everything you can to maintain a relaxed and casual atmosphere.

Your children may be suspicious at this turn of events and try to embroil you in controversy over what they like or don't like. Just stay calm but firm. Don't get involved with what they are eating. Above all, enjoy your own meal.[7]

When family situations get tense over misbehavior and discipline problems, remember the example of God's Son, Jesus, while He walked on earth. Even though everyone else wanted to throw stones at the woman who was caught in adultery, He didn't condemn her but gently told her to "sin no more." And to the thief on the cross who suddenly saw his sin, Jesus in an act of forgiveness promised him a home in heaven. Forgiveness and lack of condemnation must also be part of the way we relate to our erring children.

Home Is Where the Heart Is

When my daughter Krissy was in college, I sometimes would try to get a layover in Chicago on my business flights. If I could get one long enough, I would catch the "el" in Chicago and head for North Park College to visit her. Many times I arrived unexpectedly.

If you've been in a college dormitory lately, you may have some idea of how college students keep their rooms and how they decorate them. But I was shocked to see Krissy's room as a nineteen-year-old sophomore. First of all, her room was *not* a pigsty. It was clean as a whistle. I counted twenty-six pictures displayed in her room, and all but one were of her family. She had pictures of her brother, her sisters, her mom and dad—the entire family—literally all over her room.

What does that say about middle-child Krissy who four years earlier could barely wiggle her fingers in recognition of me at her volleyball game? What does it say about the place of family in her life? If kids feel like they belong to your family, you've given them a tremendous gift. You've given them a gift that's going to ward off a peer group who's saying to your son or daughter, "Be cool like us. Drink this, snort that, smoke that. It's good for you!" Your son or daughter will have the wherewithal to say *no* to a world that says *yes* to all kinds of destructive behaviors if you have accomplished the "B" part of the ABCs of self-esteem in children. They need to belong to your family.

Peace, order, and joy. Building strong relationships with your children is an investment that will bring you joy both now and in the future, even after they've left home. So go ahead. Relax. Enjoy your children. Remember, what does it take to turn out a great child? Not a perfect parent, but a *good* parent—someone like you.

 ■ Close the session by gathering in a circle. Stand silently, looking around at the parents you have gotten to know. Remember the situations and concerns they shared when they were together with you in small groups. Ask each person to request one thing the group can pray about as the group comes to a close. Now take time to pray. If it is useful to do it this way, pray for the family of the person to your right.
■ Afterward go to one parent and tell him or her that you will pray for that person and call him or her once a week for the next three weeks. Be sure to get a phone number, and follow through on your commitment.

Name _____ Phone _____

Answer key for the Bible study on page 204:

Results of "training in the Lord"
For parents:
1. Gladness (23:15)
2. Rejoicing (23:16)
3. Great joy (23:24)
4. Delight (23:24; 29:17)

For children:
1. Fear of the Lord (2:5)
2. Knowledge of God (2:5)
3. Guidance, protection (6:22)
4. Life (6:23)
5. Hope (19:18)
6. Wisdom (29:15)
7. Peace (29:17)

Results of no "training in the Lord"
For parents:
1. Grief (17:21,25)
2. Lack of joy (17:21)
3. Bitterness (17:25)
4. Disgrace (29:15)

For children:
1. Death (5:23; 15:10; 19:18)
2. Correction by God (15:10)
3. Folly (22:15)

Portions of this session were adapted from:

Leman, Dr. Kevin. *Bringing Up Kids Without Tearing Them Down* (chapters 3 and 11). Nashville, Tenn.: Nelson, 1995.

Leman, Dr. Kevin. *Making Children Mind Without Losing Yours* (chapters 4 and 7). Grand Rapids, Mich.: Revell, 1984.

For further information, consider:

Elkind, David. *All Grown Up and No Place to Go: Teenagers in Crisis.* Reading, Mass.: Addison-Wesley, 1984, 1998.

Elkind, *The Hurried Child: Growing Up Too Fast Too Soon.* Reading, Mass.: Addison-Wesley, 1981, 1988.

Elkind, *Understanding Your Child from Birth to Sixteen.* Boston: Allyn and Bacon, 1994.

Shenk, Sara Wenger. *Why Not Celebrate!* A collection of over 150 family activities. Intercourse, Penn.: Good Books, 1987.

NOTES

1. Adapted from Dr. Kevin Leman, *Bringing Up Children Without Tearing Them Down.* (Nashville, Tenn.: Nelson, 1995), pp. 56, 57.
2. Adapted from Dr. Kevin Leman, *Making Children Mind Without Losing Yours.* (Grand Rapids, Mich.: Revell, 1984), p. 136.
3. Adapted from Dr. Kevin Leman, *Making Children Mind . . .*, p. 75.
4. Adapted from Dr. Kevin Leman, *Bringing Up Children . . .*, pp. 327-328.
5. John Heywood's *Proverbs,* first printed in 1546, is the earliest collection of English colloquial sayings. Quoted in *Bartlett's Familiar Quotations,* 16th Edition. Boston: Little, Brown and Company, 1992, p. 141.
6. Marcus Cato, 234-149 B.C. Quoted in *Bartlett's Familiar Quotations,* 16th Edition. Boston: Little, Brown and Company, 1992, p. 743.
7. Adapted from Dr. Kevin Leman, *Making Children Mind . . .*, pp. 139-140.

More great family resources from NavPress!

Raising Adults

Are your children becoming adults or just adult-aged children?
Jim Hancock challenges assumptions and creates common
ground to allow parents to give their children the tools to accept
responsiblity and gain an adult perspective on life.

Raising Adults
(Jim Hancock) $11

Parenting Adolescents

There are some things about your teen that you
can't change—no matter how much you'd like to. Learn to
focus only on those things that are within your control.

Parenting Adolescents
(Kevin Huggins) $15

Becoming a Couple of Promise

Based on Dr. Kevin Leman's leading *Keeping the Promise* video series and
workshop, *Becoming a Couple of Promise* guides you at any stage
of marriage to maintain a relationship that lasts.

Becoming a Couple of Promise
(Dr. Kevin Leman) $10

Get your copies today at your local bookstore, or call
(800) 366-7788 and ask for offer **#2079**.

NAVPRESS
BRINGING TRUTH TO LIFE
www.navpress.org

Prices subject to change without notice.